Inside
Bush
v.
Gore

Florida Government and Politics

UNIVERSITY PRESS OF FLORIDA

Florida A&M University, Tallahassee
Florida Atlantic University, Boca Raton
Florida Gulf Coast University, Ft. Myers
Florida International University, Miami
Florida State University, Tallahassee
New College of Florida, Sarasota
University of Central Florida, Orlando
University of Florida, Gainesville
University of North Florida, Jacksonville
University of South Florida, Tampa
University of West Florida, Pensacola

Inside
Bush
V.
Gore

Charley Wells

FORMER CHIEF JUSTICE FLORIDA SUPREME COURT

University Press of Florida

Gainesville · Tallahassee · Tampa · Boca Raton

Pensacola · Orlando · Miami · Jacksonville · Ft. Myers · Sarasota

VIVA FLORIDA 500
1513–2013 | A Florida Quincentennial Book

Copyright 2013 by Charley Wells
All rights reserved
Printed in the United States of America on acid-free paper.

All Florida Supreme Court photographs by Gary Robinson and Tricia Knox.

This book may be available in an electronic edition.

18 17 16 15 14 13   6 5 4 3 2 1

Library of Congress Cataloging-in-Publication Data
Wells, Charley.
Inside Bush v. Gore / Charley Wells.
p. cm. — (Florida government and politics)
Includes index.
ISBN 978-0-8130-4475-0 (alk. paper)
1. Presidents—United States—Election—2000. 2. Bush, George W. (George
Walker), 1946—Trials, litigation, etc. 3. Gore, Albert, 1948—Trials, litigation,
etc. 4. Contested elections—United States. 5. Contested elections—Florida.
I. Title. II. Title: Inside Bush vs. Gore. III. Title: Inside Bush versus Gore.
IV. Series: Florida government and politics.
E889.W45 2013
324.973'0929—dc23
2012046693

The University Press of Florida is the scholarly publishing agency for the State
University System of Florida, comprising Florida A&M University, Florida
Atlantic University, Florida Gulf Coast University, Florida International
University, Florida State University, New College of Florida, University of
Central Florida, University of Florida, University of North Florida, University
of South Florida, and University of West Florida.

University Press of Florida
15 Northwest 15th Street
Gainesville, FL 32611-2079
http://www.upf.com

This work is dedicated to my parents, J. R. Wells and Julia Talley Wells, and to my life partner, love, and in-house counsel, Linda Fischer Wells, who always have given to me their unequivocal support and confidence, required from me honesty and integrity in all endeavors, and instilled in me an abiding faith in the law and in common sense.

Contents

Foreword

Florida has held a unique place in the American mind for more than six decades. For many retirees, its environment has been like a healthy elixir that allowed them to live longer and more vigorous lives; for others, it served as a place of renewal where all things were possible; and for immigrants, it offered political freedom and access to the American dream. Historian Gary Mormino has described Florida as a "powerful symbol of renewal and regeneration." Others have suggested that if Florida had not been available to Americans after World War II, they would have been much poorer for it. Those who watched the 2000 presidential election unfold, however, wondered if that were in fact so.

During World War II, Americans from all walks of life discovered Florida through military service, and it opened their eyes to the state's postwar possibilities. With the end of the war in August 1945, Florida veterans returned home, where they were soon joined by hundreds and then thousands of Americans who were ready to pursue a new life in the Sunshine State. In the sixty-five years between 1945 and 2010, 17 million people moved to Florida, increasing the state's population to 18.8 million people in 2005.

Florida's population growth and the settlement patterns and diversity of its new residents had a profound effect on the state's place in the nation as well as upon the image Floridians had of themselves. Prior to 1940, Florida had the smallest population in the South and was one of the poorest states in the nation. Its society and economy were rural and agricultural, biracial and segregated. Most residents resided within forty miles of the Georgia border, and their culture and politics were consequently southern in orientation. Like its southern neighbors, Florida was a one-party state, with the Democratic Party dominating politics from the end of Reconstruction in 1876 to 1970.

All that changed in the fifty-plus years following World War II. In less than an average life span today, Florida became by 2010 the most populous state in the region and the fourth-most-populous in the nation, a haven for seniors and foreign residents that boasts a dynamic multiracial and multiethnic culture. Most Floridians now reside closer to the Caribbean than they do to Georgia, and, for most of them, their image of themselves and their state has changed dramatically to reflect this new geographic orientation.

As Florida changed, so too did its politics. Voters threw out the Constitution of 1885 in favor of a new document that would speak to the needs of a modern state in 1968. They then gradually abandoned the Democratic Party in favor of a dynamic two-party system. By the 1990s, Republicans took their expanding constituency and their control of the districting process following the 1990 U.S. Census to secure majorities in the state legislature and the congressional delegation. These were remarkable political developments and reflected the transformative changes in the state's population. However, in statewide races for governor, U.S. senator, and elected cabinet positions, as well as in presidential contests, Democrats remained competitive with their Republican counterparts, in large part because they held a 6 percent lead in registered voters (42 percent to 36 percent for Republicans).

Such a politically and demographically complex and diverse population has made Florida today something other than a unified whole. The political maxim that "all politics is local" is truer of Florida than of most other states. For example, those who reside in north Florida share little in common with those living in central or south Florida and vice versa. While those residing in southeast Florida see themselves as part of the "new America," those in north Florida view Miami as a foreign country. Ask a resident what it means to be a Floridian, and few, if any, can answer the question. Ask a Floridian about the state's history, and even fewer can tell you that it has operated under five different flags or that its colonial period began much earlier than that of New England or Virginia. Perhaps one in ten or twenty can tell you who Democrat

LeRoy Collins was, despite Republican Jeb Bush's acknowledgment of Collins as the model for all governors who followed him. It is literally a state unknown and indefinable to its people. Such historical ignorance and regional division become major obstacles when state leaders try to find consensus among voters and solutions that address the needs of all citizens.

An essential purpose of this series is to put Floridians in touch with their rich and diverse history and to enhance their understanding of the political developments that have shaped and reshaped the state, region, and nation. This series focuses on the Sunshine State's unique and fascinating political history since 1900 and on public policy issues that have influenced the state and nation. The University Press of Florida is dedicated to producing high-quality books on these subjects. It is also committed to publishing shorter essays of twenty-five to fifty pages in this series that address some of the immediately pressing public policy issues confronting Florida. As part of this series, the University Press of Florida also welcomes book manuscripts on the region that examine critical political and policy developments that impacted Florida.

In this volume, former Florida Supreme Court chief justice Charles T. Wells takes us inside the courtroom to reexamine the highly contested presidential election of 2000. Wells offers an extremely valuable account of the hotly disputed election of 2000 in Florida that is not available anywhere else. Wells was at the center of the controversy, heading a Supreme Court that had to come to grips with numerous problems in the state election laws and ultimately decide the outcome of one of the closest presidential elections in American history. In the process, he provides a detailed analysis of the problems in Florida's election laws at the time and how the court decided to handle them.

Wells has refrained from assessing the discussion and decisions of his fellow jurists because to do so would violate his position on the court. In this regard, readers may be disappointed, but the chief justice has laid out his own thinking and the basis for it. That in itself makes this book exceedingly valuable for those of us who are fascinated by this election and the result.

The Bush margin of victory was a mere 537 votes in Florida, which would not only decide the outcome in the state, but also determine the presidential election. Compared to this mere handful of ballots were a whopping 175,010 ballots that were not counted by vote-tabulating machines and that came largely from Democratic-rich urban areas in south and central Florida. The Gore team pushed hard to get the state courts and the Florida Supreme Court to count these votes, but the Bush team argued that there were too many problems with these ballots to determine the intent of the voters who cast them.

With the presidential election at stake, with so many ballots in disarray, and with a judicial process unsuited to rapid and timely decisions, there was tremendous pressure on the justices to decide matters and do so quickly. Wells tells this side of the story extremely well, and many will be fascinated by the insight he offers into the daily work schedule of the justices and their efforts to move quickly but also thoughtfully through this crisis.

In its final decision on December 8, 2000, the Florida Supreme Court, by a 4–3 vote, with Wells voting with the minority, ordered a statewide manual recount. A day later, the U.S. Supreme Court, by a 5–4 vote, overturned the Florida Supreme Court and, by this decision, effectively halted the process, ensuring Bush's election as the forty-third president of the United States. It was high political and judicial drama at its most meaningful.

From Wells's perspective, the hanging chads in punch-card ballots were the crux of the matter, and it was impossible to produce more accurate results by manually inspecting and counting the votes by hand. As Wells writes: "Overlaying all of the practical problems was my realization that regardless of how much more counting was done, or what was eventually ordered by our court or by the U.S. Supreme Court, or done by the Florida legislature or Congress, there would not be any more certainty of the correctness of the vote count. At this point I concluded that after all the counting was done, the margin of error was always going to be greater than the margin of victory."

Many readers will take issue with Wells's conclusion, and many will express concern that Wells's decision seemed grounded in politics rather than in the law. But the chief justice makes an exceedingly effective case for his position, and students of this election will be fascinated with his role in this process and how he came to his conclusions.

This is a spellbinding story and even more so because it is told by the chief justice at the center of the crisis. Wells recounts his view of events dispassionately and thoughtfully. It is a must-read for Floridians and for scholars and students of state politics who are fascinated by this election, its outcome, and its significance for the nation.

David R. Colburn and Susan A. MacManus
Series editors

Inside
Bush
v.
Gore

Opening Statement

Like millions of Americans, on the morning of November 7, 2000, I cast my vote for the forty-third president of the United States. As I drove away from the polls, my duty done, I thought my role in the election was over. It certainly did not cross my mind that I would quickly be swept into the center of a tension-filled national controversy. But, as chief justice of the Florida Supreme Court, my role had just begun. It was only the first day of the tumultuous thirty-six-day period it would take to determine the presidency.

At home that night, my wife, Linda, and I followed the early returns. The vote was close in all sections of the country, and particularly in Florida. Surprisingly, early in the evening, the television networks reported that Vice President Al Gore had won Florida. I was skeptical.

For the week before the election, television and newspaper commentators had predicted Gore could win the state. I thought a Gore victory was unlikely. In my experience, Florida, dating from the first time I voted in a presidential election in 1960, had leaned toward the Republican candidate.

Despite early television network projections that Gore had won Florida, I saw Gore's narrow lead in the early precinct returns as a favorable indicator for Texas governor George W. Bush. The polls in the Florida Panhandle were in the Central Time Zone and had not yet closed. They did not close until an hour after the rest of the state. I knew the conservative Panhandle would be a Bush stronghold.

Between 8:30 and 9:00 that night, the networks withdrew their calls that Gore had won Florida. This made more sense. Linda and I watched the returns on television until around 10:00 p.m. and then turned on our portable radios, trying to go to sleep.

Before I turned off the radio at 11:30 p.m., the newscaster announced that Bush was ahead by 246 votes and that, based upon the projected electoral winners in other states, the winner of the presidency would likely be decided by the outcome of the vote in Florida. As I fell asleep, I thought the election would not be decided until the next day, and it would likely be decided by absentee ballots.

I awoke at approximately 2:00 a.m. Linda, who was still listening to her portable radio, said, "They've called Florida for Bush." I responded that I didn't think that was possible either since the absentee votes weren't in yet. Five minutes later, Linda reported, "They again pulled Florida from having been decided." I thought to myself—similar to the way astronauts on Apollo 13 assessed their situation—"Houston, we've got a problem."

The next morning it was even more apparent that the outcome of the presidential election would hinge on Florida. At that time, I began to realize that the Florida Supreme Court would be drawn into the battle.

While I then understood that the Florida Supreme Court would be at the center of the election fight, I did not know at the time—nor is it likely that many others knew—how little time the U.S. Code in title 3, section 5 provided for Florida to finally resolve the dispute. Even more than a decade after *Bush v. Gore*, one of its most overlooked lessons is the need to reform the U.S. code timeline for a state determining the presidential victor in a close election.

The final outcome of the election in Florida took thirty-six days. What is usually missed in discussions about *Bush v. Gore* is that thirty-six days was what the parties agreed was the maximum time available for a final resolution by Florida of the controversies as to who was the winner of Florida's electoral votes.

The first question I asked of the lawyers for both Governor Bush and Vice President Gore during the oral argument before the Florida Supreme Court on November 20, 2000, was when all controversies had to be finally resolved in order for Florida's presidential electors not to be prejudiced as to participation in the presidential Electoral College. The lawyers answered, December 12, 2000.

This is an extremely short period of time to resolve the legally interwoven federal and state controversies inherent in a disputed presidential election. The resolution within this time span was certain to leave the losing candidate, that candidate's supporters, and many commentators, observers, and historians feeling that the issues were not dealt with properly or completely.

However, I came away from the experience in 2000 believing that a short period in which to resolve such controversies is necessary for the health of our democracy and representative form of government. It is elementary that power is bestowed by our citizens upon our leaders only temporarily, and is to be periodically passed to other leaders. Uncertainty as to the passing of power quickly leads to instability, which is detrimental to the societal and economic health of not only our country but of an interconnected world.

After thirty-two days of process in the 2000 controversy, it was apparent to me that the point had been reached at which it was more important to identify a winner than to continue the legal process in search of a winner. The winner, the next president, was determined four days later. I recognize that many were dissatisfied with the outcome and the reasons stated for the process ending. Yet, power did pass peacefully. The dispute came to end, and our country and our world were able to move forward.

Such finality was not clear on that thirty-second day of the controversy. On that day, December 8, 2000, a majority of the Florida Supreme Court ruled that a statewide recount of undervotes should take place.

From that ruling, I dissented. I wrote in my dissent—and continue to believe as I write this book—that had the majority's decision not been overturned by the U.S. Supreme Court, a constitutional crisis not previously seen in our nation's history would likely have resulted.

The decision by the U.S. Supreme Court has been the subject of much commentary and substantial criticism as to the constitutional theories upon which that decision was based. In this book I do not address the substance of the U.S. Supreme Court's majority opinion issued the evening of December 12, 2000. Rather, I focus on my experience from inside the Florida Supreme Court during those thirty-six days. As I realized more and more with each passing day during that period, and in the years that have followed, it was a unique and pivotal historic experience in the life of our state, our country, and certainly in my life.

My conclusion is that by December 12, 2000, what was crucial was that the U.S. Supreme Court resolved sufficient issues that a winner of the election was known. The resolution of the winner was far more important than the reasons written by the justices on the U.S. Supreme Court for that resolution.

In the thirty-six days, the Florida Supreme Court, state courts throughout Florida, federal district courts, the U.S. Court of Appeals, Eleventh Circuit, and, ultimately, the U.S. Supreme Court sorted through hundreds of disputes. These disputes involved inconsistent statutes, imperfect ballots, unclear and incomplete punch cards, and an obscure hundred-year-old opinion of the U.S. Supreme Court.

For thirty-six days, our court was on an increasingly tense roller-coaster ride, with the eyes of the world watching. It was a controversy that determined the leader of the world's most powerful democracy.

In the pages that follow, I narrate what I witnessed and experienced inside Florida's highest court. My narration is necessarily from my personal perspective, which is colored by my background and experience. I set out relevant parts of this background and experience in the first pages. I set out my reactions and thinking as events transpired day after day. My intent and hope is that this will add to the historic understanding of these thirty-six days. However, as is evident in reading the book, I have not quoted other members of the Florida Supreme Court as to what was said in conferences or in conversations between individual justices. I have included no such discussions because of the ethical obligation I had as a member of the court to preserve the confidentiality of those discussions. I respect that confidentiality. I believe it is necessary for members of appellate courts to have candid discussions of issues being deliberated. Apprehension about what is said in those discussions being made public would have a seriously debilitating effect on those discussions to the detriment of appellate decision making.

1

Preliminary Matters

On July 1, 2000, I became chief justice of the Florida Supreme Court. The position of chief justice is rotated every two years to the most senior justice who has not previously served as chief. I had been appointed to the court six years earlier by the late governor Lawton Chiles. My route to the court was through my career as a lawyer. Although I had early aspirations to be a politician, my vocation had been the law and my family.

When I graduated from law school in 1964, my primary interest was finding a way to actively engage in political campaigns. I registered as a Democrat, and I had great interest in pursuing elective office, as a legislator or even as governor.

Before I could enter politics, though, I knew I had to earn a living. I became a lawyer as so many in my family had done and continue to do. My grandfather had been a lawyer and a county judge in west Florida's Panhandle from 1900 to 1909. Additionally, my father, J. R. Wells, his brother Maxwell, my older brother, Joel, and my cousin Maxwell Jr. were all lawyers. My wife, Linda, is a lawyer as are two of my children, our son Talley and our daughter Ashley. Only our daughter Shelley escaped the legal web by becoming a doctor.

I attended the University of Florida and received my law degree in December 1964. I was best described as a "good, but not an excellent student." While I spent more time working in campus politics than I did in the law library, I did study enough to achieve one of the top three grades of candidates taking the Florida Bar examination in the spring of 1965.

Immediately thereafter I began practicing as a trial lawyer in the firm that bore the name of my dad and my uncle, Maguire, Voorhis & Wells in Orlando.

Not long after joining my family's law firm, I worked in the U.S. Senate campaign of former governor LeRoy Collins, a man I much admired. He had served as director of the Civil Rights Commission and joined Martin Luther King's march in Selma, Alabama. In his Senate campaign, Collins was labeled a "liberal integrationist"—not a popular depiction with Florida voters in 1968. Collins lost to Republican congressman Ed Gurney—part of the Republican political tide sweeping Florida and the South.

Linda also had a lifelong interest in politics dating to her childhood. She grew up in Clearwater, in Pinellas County. Her parents were active in Republican politics. Her mother and father moved to Florida from Pennsylvania in the late 1940s, and were among the post–World War II organizers of the Republican Party in that part of Florida. During the twentieth century until the end of World War II in 1945, all of Florida, including Pinellas County, was heavily Democratic. Linda's dad, as a Republican, was elected chairman of the Pinellas County Commission from 1952 to 1960. He was one of the first Republican officeholders in Florida since Reconstruction. Linda's mother was a Republican delegate to the Republican National Convention during Eisenhower's presidency. Despite her Republican upbringing, Linda became a Democrat after college.

Linda and I married in late 1969, and she moved to Orlando, where she practiced law and became active in the local Democratic Party serving as president of the Orange County Democratic Women's Club.

In 1970, I ran for a seat in the Florida House of Representatives as a Democrat. I lost to a very nice retired U.S. Army colonel from Winter Park, Florida, who was an obscure two-term Republican incumbent. I found being a political candidate much more difficult than I had envisioned. Maybe this was because I was a Democrat caught in a Republican stampede. I remained registered as a Democrat because it seemed to me that the rise of the Republicans in central Florida was driven by political stances that were opposed to integration and civil rights, which were causes I strongly supported. Nonetheless, the loss stung me, and my 1970 campaign was my one and only attempt at elective office.

Instead, I settled comfortably into being a father, a husband, and an attorney, which I found quite satisfying. I became actively involved in the Orange County Bar Association, later becoming its president, and was named to the state bar's Board of Governors. I stayed connected to statewide politics and took leadership roles in the campaigns of Reubin Askew and Lawton Chiles for governor. Both were Democrats.

I did continue to have an interest in serving in government, and from time to time considered the possibility of seeking an appointment to be a judge. Even though I certainly recognized the difficulties in starting my judicial service at the top of the state judiciary, I was particularly attracted to serving on the Florida Supreme Court. During my legal career, the court repeatedly considered and decided important issues confronting Florida's fast-growing, dynamic, and diverse population. I noted that few important legal or political issues arose anywhere in the United States that did not quickly find their way to the Florida Supreme Court.

The appointment process to the Supreme Court is referred to as "merit selection." When there is a vacancy on the court, the governor has to appoint a replacement from a list of three nominees selected by a nominating commission. In 1994, Justice Parker Lee McDonald, who was from the geographical area that included Orlando, reached the mandatory retirement age under the Florida Constitution for a judge, which is seventy years. His successor also had to be, at the time of appointment, a resident of the Orlando area. The vacancy came at a point in my career when I had been a trial lawyer for twenty-nine years; our children were in college, and at age fifty-five, I could comfortably give up my law practice. I applied for appointment to the Supreme Court. I believed my lengthy and substantial experience as a trial and appellate lawyer was the type of background needed by the Supreme Court at that time. The court had no member who had recent experience as a lawyer. Even though I had not previously been a judge at any level, my work with the state and local lawyers' associations and friendships made in that work helped me to be selected for the list of three to fill the vacancy on the Supreme Court. The chair of the nominating commission,

John Frost, was a particularly good friend. Of the three nominees selected by the nominating commission, I was the only practicing lawyer; the two others were active judges, members of the Fifth District Court of Appeals. Both were well qualified and would have served the court well.

After being selected as one of the three nominees from whom the appointment had to be made, I was undoubtedly helped in the appointment process by the fact that Governor Chiles and I had a history dating back to his first campaign for the U.S. Senate in 1970. Nicknamed "Walking Lawton," he had walked 1,033 miles in that campaign, from Florida's Panhandle to the Keys, wearing out dozens of pairs of army-style boots. He limited his campaign contributions to one hundred dollars. Chiles was affable, folksy, perhaps best described as down-to-earth. He and I met at a Winter Park function in the middle of July 1970 during his first Senate run. He told me he was "walking" the next day to Kissimmee, approximately fifteen miles away. I did not tell him, but I thought that that was the craziest thing I had ever heard. If nothing else, the road from Orlando to Kissimmee is broiling in the Florida sun in July. Crazy as it was, Lawton Chiles's walkathon caught the voters' fancy. Florida's voters liked Chiles, and he won the U.S. Senate seat. After serving in the Senate, he was elected in 1990 to be Florida's governor, and was a very popular governor. I had stayed in contact with Governor Chiles over the intervening years, and Linda and I had become friends with his daughter, who lived in Orlando.

While my friendship over the years with Governor Chiles and his family helped me in my appointment to the court, I believe that the political views I held at the time of my appointment played little or no role. When Governor Chiles interviewed me before naming me to the court, we never discussed politics or controversial issues such as abortion or the death penalty that would likely come before the court. Nor did Governor Chiles ask how I felt about the court's role in the government.

Instead, during our fifteen-minute meeting, the governor and I reminisced about our past contacts and how well our children were doing. This always impressed me. By not bringing up a single current issue that could come before the court, the governor reflected the experience and wisdom of his long years of service in both the federal and state governments. He showed that he respected the necessarily independent role of the judicial branch, and that what he was interested in considering in a nominee for the Supreme Court was the character, personal history, and personality of a nominee. That was what would be important for the future of the judiciary, not the nominee's views about some transient, politically charged issue. Governor Chiles knew that issues come and go, but judicial appointments last forever—or, in Florida, until age seventy. Although appellate judges in Florida are required to be on the ballot for a retention vote every six years through the year 2000, no Supreme Court justice had received less than 60 percent of the votes for retention.

When I was appointed to the court, Linda and I both withdrew from all political activities. We maintained, though, a serious interest in elections and campaigns as observers and students of politics and government. In Florida, being a judge or justice is a nonpartisan position. The Florida Judicial Code of Conduct does not permit active judges or justices to engage in election activities except in their own elections or retentions. I was a political free agent, and, in the appointment process, Governor Chiles had not made any attempt to inhibit that free agency.

Before I was appointed to the Florida Supreme Court, my legal work, during the almost thirty years I was a lawyer, was exclusively in civil law. I was primarily involved in personal-injury claims and insurance issues. Upon joining the court, I was immediately immersed in criminal cases weighted with a heavy load of capital cases. Florida's legislature had reenacted the death penalty for first-degree murder in 1974, and the statute had passed constitutional muster in both the U.S. Supreme Court and the Florida Supreme Court in 1976. By the time of my appointment to the court in 1994, death penalty cases dominated the docket of the Florida Supreme Court.

When I arrived at the court, the number of inmates on death row in Florida prisons exceeded 350. Many of those inmates had been sentenced to death in the 1970s, and their cases proceeded slowly in Florida's state and federal courts. Pursuant to Florida's constitution, all cases in which defendants are sentenced to death are appealed directly from the trial court to the Florida Supreme Court. Almost every other type of case is appealed from the trial court to a district court of appeal and only after a review and written opinion in that appellate court to the Florida Supreme Court, which then has discretion to accept or deny review. Capital cases that are affirmed by the Florida Supreme Court proceed to postconviction review in both the state court and the federal court system. Post-conviction review in capital cases added as much as the direct appeals to the workload of the Florida Supreme Court.

Criminal cases that reached the Florida Supreme Court generally raised constitutional issues under both the state and federal constitutions. This was particularly the situation in capital cases.

During my first six years, I also did a great deal of research into the specifics of the processing of individual death-penalty cases pending in the Florida Supreme Court and in the Florida trial courts. I wanted to understand why those cases took so long from trial to being finally adjudicated. I was very concerned about the length of time inmates were maintained on death row, which is a special and very limiting type of confinement. As I wrote in 1998 in *Knight v. State*,[1] I agreed with U.S. Supreme Court Justice Stephen Breyer's dissenting opinion in *Ellege v. Florida* stating that such confinement for years, because of its length and unique pressures, could become cruel and unusual punishment.[2] I thought the state had an obligation to have the inmate's case processed within a reasonable period of time so that the inmate would either be executed or removed from that type of confinement.

Another interest that I pursued during these years was building relationships with some of the leaders in the legislature. While I was committed to the doctrine of separation of powers of the executive, legislative, and judicial branches of government, and to the necessity in our democracy and representative government for an independent judiciary, I found it to be increasingly important for the proper functioning of Florida's government for there to be more reciprocal respect by the leadership of each branch for the separate powers of all three

---

1   746 So.2d 423, 439–440 (Fla. 1998) (Wells concurring in part, dissenting in part).
2   525 U.S. 944, 119 S. Ct. 366 (1998) (Breyer dissenting).

branches of the government. In both my judicial opinions and in personal contacts, I worked to foster a better relationship by what I wrote and said. I considered the appearance of a lack of joint respect to be a significant problem in Florida's government.

During these years, however, contrary to the better relationship I had hoped I could help build for the court with the legislative leadership, debilitating tension increased between the legislature and the court centered upon capital cases. The legislative leadership was increasingly critical of the length of time in the processing of capital cases and attributed the delays to Florida's courts. My work in trying to understand what was causing those cases to go on so long and my opinions criticizing the delays did permit me to have a better relationship with those leaders than did the court as a whole. But by early 2000, the relationship between the legislative leaders, particularly in the House of Representatives, was not good.

In the fall of 1999 and the early months of 2000, a wide breach developed when the court reviewed and ruled upon the reforms the legislature adopted in the Death Penalty Reform Act. The court ruled that act to be unconstitutional under the Florida Constitution because the act encroached upon the court's power to set procedures for the processing of cases through Florida's courts. The opinion in a case styled *Allen v. Butterworth* issued in April 2000 was written by the then chief justice Major Harding,[3] and rested upon the court's precedent construing the sections of the Florida Constitution mandating separation of powers and providing the Supreme Court the power to set the procedural rules for cases in Florida's courts. I recognized that the decision was going to exacerbate the tension with the legislative leadership, but the opinion was correct, and I joined in the unanimous decision.

Further tension between the legislature and the court arose before the 2000 presidential election from the court's September 2000 decision involving another death-penalty case, *Armstrong v. Harris.*[4] In that case, the court struck from the Florida Constitution a provision concerning the death penalty that had been placed by the legislature on the

---

3   756 So.2d 52 (Fla. 2000).
4   773 So.2d 7 (Fla. 2000).

election ballot in 1998 and approved by a substantial majority of voters. I did believe that the court's majority went too far in that decision, and that the majority opinion used too strident language in reference to the legislature. I did not join the majority, instead writing a lengthy dissent.[5]

Thus, on November 7, 2000, when the election controversy began, there was a history of recent substantial tension, animosity, and suspicion in the relationship between our court and the legislative leadership, especially with the House of Representatives. This was the unfortunate seedbed in which the presidential election controversy was to grow.

---

5   *Id.* at 26 (Wells dissenting).

2

The Day after the Election

When I arrived at the court on the day after the election, the lead story in the *Tallahassee Democrat* was headlined, in all caps, "It's President Bush," but the *Ft. Lauderdale Sun Sentinel* from Broward County declared, "Cliffhanger . . . Up in the Air: Bush-Gore." The *Palm Beach Post* simply said, "Bush, For Now."

The *Post* also reported on an emerging conflict regarding so-called "butterfly ballots," which had names in two columns with punch holes in between the columns. It was a confusing ballot and made it difficult for voters to choose the candidates they preferred.

That day the court went through routine business amid growing discussion among my colleagues about the direction the election was heading. Later that day, Tom Hall, the clerk of the Supreme Court, came into my office and gave me a heads-up that he had received a call saying that litigation was being prepared regarding the ballots in Palm Beach County and that he expected a case would be filed soon. I appreciated the information. I had come to the conclusion that our justices would be far better prepared to process cases if they knew about issues that were coming our way.

I wanted to find out quickly what, if anything, election statutes said about the form of a ballot. I examined the statutes but could not find any provision that would prohibit the ballot used in Palm Beach County.

By midafternoon, the media reported Bush leading by approximately 1,700 votes. It was unclear whether this included absentee ballots. Around this time, one of my law clerks, Hunter Carroll, came into my office and advised me that there could be an issue involving what were being referred to as "overseas ballots." These were absentee ballots cast by voters who for various reasons were domiciled outside of the United States, and mainly included those serving in the military. Hunter advised me that the overseas ballots probably were not due to be received in the offices of the county supervisors of elections until ten days following an election. This news sent me back again to the election statutes, and I could find no provision in the statutes that authorized the ten-day period. I asked Hunter and my other law clerks to dig further to find out the legal basis for the ten-day period and how that worked with the other deadlines for votes being certified as set out in the election statutes.[1]

Law clerks are essential to the work of appellate judges and were essential to the justices at the Florida Supreme Court. In 2000, each justice had three clerks and a judicial assistant. Fortunately for me, in November 2000 I had three talented and energetic clerks—Candy Slimon, Hunter Carroll, and Eric Hernandez—all recent law school graduates. Candy, the senior law clerk, was in her second year while Hunter and Eric had graduated from law school and joined my office in June 2000. My judicial assistant was Pam Stewart. Pam had been with me since I was appointed to the court in 1994 and was the cog that made my office function well every day, especially during the election crisis. As chief justice, I had two additional judicial assistants, Pat Madden and Nancy Shuford, who handled administrative matters. The entire staff pitched in as we undertook the burden of dealing with this fast-developing legal crisis.

---

1   Florida agreed with the U.S. Department of Justice in 1982 for the entry of a consent judgment allowing the ten-day period in order to comply with the Overseas Citizens Voting Rights Act of 1975, as amended in 1978. The consent judgment covered the federal elections in Florida in 1982, with the legislature required to adopt a statutory revision. The revision never expressly made it into the statutes, but the revision did make it into the Florida Administrative Code (Fl. Admin. Code Ann, r.1S-2.013) and was accepted without dispute as governing the 2000 presidential election. See Mitchell W. Berger and Candice D. Tobin, *Election 2000: The Law of Tied Presidential Elections*, 26 NOVA L. REV., 647, 671, Spring 2002, for an excellent explanation of the development of this law.

The overseas-ballot issue puzzled me. If the overseas ballots were not due for ten days, then the final election result could not be certified until ten days had passed. On the other hand, there were news reports that all the returns had to be into the State Election Commission, which was chaired by the Florida secretary of state, in no more than seven days. The plot was thickening.

3

The Florida Justices

As the presidential election controversy unfolded and made its way to our court during the next few weeks, the general public would come to know the Florida's Supreme Court in ways it had not previously. In part, this would happen as a result of a decision by the court two decades earlier, when it agreed to allow cameras into the proceedings. That was fortuitous in the court's processing of the 2000 presidential election cases. In watching oral arguments, the public would see the court's work firsthand.

I think that opening the court to television and the Internet was a very positive step. It has long been my view that courts, especially appellate courts, are too insular. I believe that it adds to confidence in court decisions when the public can witness the process in which the decisions are made. I also believe it enhances judicial preparation and decorum when the judges know that they are being seen outside of the courtroom. The courts are the public's courts, not the lawyers' or judges' courts, and public access to their courts should be facilitated when technology is available to properly do that.

Prior to *Bush v. Gore*, however, the general public knew relatively little about our court or its members, past or present. The only significant media coverage of the court other than the broadcasting of the oral arguments had been in the early 1970s, when three of the justices were accused of various acts of misconduct. This low level of public scrutiny was about to change.

As the coverage of the election controversy began, the media labeled Justices Lee Shaw, Harry Anstead, Barbara Pariente, and Fred Lewis as moderates.[1]

This was not my experience. In my opinion, Justices Shaw, Anstead, Pariente, and Lewis were philosophically liberal as that label is used in contemporary political commentary. Justice Peggy Quince was more moderate than the other four, but often joined them in decisions. Justice Major Harding and I were more consistently conservative.

The use of the labels "liberal" and "conservative" is inherently ambiguous and, of course, in the mind of the beholder. My use of the labels in respect to the justices is related to their views in deciding cases. In respect to constitutional issues and the power of the judicial branch relative to the legislative and executive branches of the government, liberal justices are more likely to find expansive individual rights and to assert the power of the judicial branch over the other two branches of the government. In criminal cases, liberal justices consistently find more ways to rule in favor of the accused and against the State than conservative justices. In civil cases, a liberal justice is more likely to find theories that support claims for the recovery of money in cases involving personal injuries and damages than a conservative justice.

The senior justice was Leander Shaw, whom we called Lee. Appointed by Governor Bob Graham in 1983, Lee Shaw was the second African American to serve on the court since Reconstruction, and the first to serve as chief justice. Justice Shaw, whose father had been dean of the Florida A&M Graduate School, graduated from West Virginia State College and then received a law degree from Howard University in 1957. He began his legal career in Jacksonville in the Offices of the Public Defender and the State Attorney.

Although Justice Shaw was involved in the civil rights movement in northeast Florida in the 1960s and 1970s, I never heard him discuss what he did except for commenting, from time to time, on the difficulties that he and others had representing protestors who had taken part in sit-in demonstrations in St. Augustine. Growing up in the segregated

---

1   *Orlando Sentinel*, November 20, 2000, A-6.

South and being actively involved in the civil rights tumult of the 1960s and 1970s were, of course, experiences that Justice Shaw brought with him as a judge and later as a justice.

In the 1970s, Justice Shaw was appointed to the board that administered workers' compensation claims, then to the Florida Court of Appeals, and finally to the Florida Supreme Court. I did not know Justice Shaw personally when I came on the court, but I quickly developed great respect for him and found him to be open, straightforward, and well informed. Justice Shaw wrote some of the most widely referenced cases decided by the court.

Examples of Justice Shaw's majority opinions include *State v. DiGuillo*, which established the harmless-error analysis to be used in Florida criminal cases.[2] Harmless-error analysis begins from the widely accepted jurisprudential premise that there are few, if any, trials in which some legal error is not committed. Convicted criminal defendants obviously maintain that any error is harmful and should result in their convictions being reversed. The U.S. Supreme Court, however, has differentiated between trial errors that necessitate retrials of cases, and trial errors that, while recognized as errors, are determined not to have harmed (affected) the outcome in the case. Justice Shaw's opinion established a standard for such error in Florida cases that has proven to be friendlier to criminal defendants than the standard established by the U.S. Supreme Court. This is the harmless-error analysis that continues to be applied in Florida courts.

Along a similar line, Justice Shaw wrote an opinion 1992 in *Traylor v. State* that held that the Florida Constitution could place more rigorous restraints on governmental intrusion into individual rights than found in the U.S. Constitution, but could not place more restraints on individual rights than allowed by the U.S. Constitution.[3] Justice Shaw wrote an opinion in 1989 holding Florida's Parental Notification Act regarding minors' abortions unconstitutional based upon the Florida Constitution. He was the author of the four-member majority opinion in *Armstrong v. Harris* that evoked substantial negative comment by the

---

2   491 So.2d 1129 (Fla. 1986).
3   596 So.2d 957 (Fla. 1992).

legislative leadership.[4] Most reviewers would consider these opinions to be philosophically liberal.

The next-most-senior member was Major Harding, appointed by Governor Chiles in 1991. Justice Harding grew up in North Carolina and graduated from Wake Forest. After law school, he served in the U.S. Army, and later was appointed judge of the juvenile court for Duval County, and then in 1970 was appointed to the circuit court. At the time of his appointment to the Florida Supreme Court, Justice Harding had served more than twenty years as a trial judge and was widely respected and liked by trial judges from all over Florida. Justice Harding was gregarious, a leader in his church and active in Tallahassee civic activities, and was distinctive for another reason—he always wore a bow tie.

Justice Harding and I worked closely during his two years as chief justice of the court. As I stated, we spent a great deal of time and effort trying to build relationships with the legislative leadership. Justice Harding and his wife, Jane, became close friends with Linda and me. Justice Harding was mostly conservative in both his theology and his jurisprudence. He did though write the opinion in *Allen v. Butterworth*[5] holding the Death Penalty Reform Act unconstitutional and joined with the majority in *Armstrong v. Harris*.[6]

I was the third-most-senior member.

I was followed in seniority by Harry Anstead, who had also been appointed by Governor Chiles in 1994. Justice Anstead and I were law-school classmates. He grew up in Jacksonville in poverty. The youngest of six children, he was raised by a single mother. Following law school, Justice Anstead joined a small firm in West Palm Beach and was active in the local Democratic Party in Palm Beach County. After joining the Supreme Court, he often spoke to visiting groups who from time to time toured the court of his life growing up in the "projects," which plainly had a substantial impact on the views he brought to his work as a judge. An event that he also often recounted as very meaningful in his formative experiences was being present in 1961 in Washington, D.C., at the inauguration of President John F. Kennedy, whom he greatly

---

4   773 So.2d 7 (Fla. 2000).
5   756 So.2d 52 (Fla. 2000).
6   773 So.2d 7 (Fla. 2000).

admired, and whose inaugural address plainly made a lasting impression on him.

In 1977, Justice Anstead was appointed to the Florida Court of Appeals for the Fourth District, which is located in West Palm Beach. He served there until being named to the Supreme Court in 1994. Justice Anstead was a "quick study," and often incisive in legal matters. By 2000, I had little doubt that "liberal" was an appropriate label for him. I found that as a justice he had strong views in support of an expansive, strong role for the judiciary relative to the legislative and executive branches of government, and as to the constitutional rights of criminal defendants. His was a hard vote for the State to get in criminal cases. In civil cases, he generally favored claimants recovering money from their defendants. Early in our time on the court, I came to understand that Justice Anstead was a devotee of the opinions and activism of the U.S. Supreme Court during the period in which that Court was led by Chief Justice Earl Warren. This was a devotion that I only partially shared.

Though we had been undergraduates and in law school at the University of Florida at the same time, Justice Anstead and I had not stayed in contact after graduating from law school. We were not personally or philosophically close during our time on the court.

The fifth-most-senior justice was Barbara Pariente, a native of New York City and a graduate of Boston University and George Washington Law School. She had a clerkship with United States District Court Judge Norman Roettger in the Southern District of Florida, and then joined a firm in West Palm Beach headed by veteran and widely respected plaintiff personal-injury lawyer Al Cone. She later founded a small firm with another lawyer, primarily representing plaintiffs in personal-injury claims. She was appointed to the Florida Court of Appeals for the Fourth District by Governor Chiles in 1993, and then to the Supreme Court in 1997. I knew Justice Pariente casually prior to her appointment, but I was not very familiar with her work.

When she became a member of the court, I found her to be very bright, energetic, and hardworking. However, it was not long after her appointment that she made clear to me that she and I had very different views on many issues of both criminal and civil law. What she said proved to be true. In my opinion, she never let go of her experience as a claimant's attorney. In almost every case involving insurance, she was for the claimant and against the insurance company. Similar to Justice Anstead in deciding constitutional issues involving individual rights, she was committed to liberal views that traced to the era of Chief Justice Earl Warren's U.S. Supreme Court holdings. I thought that often in oral arguments she and Justice Anstead voiced hostility toward defendants in civil cases and the State in criminal cases. She favored an active and dominant role for the court relative to the legislative and executive branches.

Justices Anstead and Pariente had served together for a couple of years on the Fourth District Court of Appeals before Justice Anstead was appointed to the Supreme Court. During the time Justice Pariente had been a member of the Supreme Court, her views aligned with Justice Anstead and she voted consistently with Justice Anstead in cases. Her appointment changed the balance of the court from a 4–3 conservative majority to a 4–3 liberal majority (which became a 5–2 liberal majority when Justices Lewis and Quince joined the court). Examples of this are seen in the many criminal cases in which Justices Anstead and Pariente voiced an expansive view of the Fourth and Fifth Amendments of the U.S. Constitution. They comprised two members of the four-justice majority in *Armstrong v. Harris*.[7]

The sixth-most-senior justice, Fred Lewis, appointed by Governor Chiles in 1998, was born and reared in Beckley, West Virginia, and attended Florida Southern College on an athletic grant-in-aid. Upon graduation he earned his law degree from the University of Miami Law School in 1972. After military service, Justice Lewis entered private practice in Miami, handling civil trial and appellate litigation, at which he reportedly excelled. A very significant event in Justice Lewis's life had been and was the severely debilitating illness of his youngest daughter, to whom Justice Lewis and his wife, Judy, were totally committed and devoted. Like me, Justice Lewis had not served as a judge before he was appointed to the court.

When he joined the court, I found Justice Lewis to be exceptionally intelligent and attentive to detail, but by November 2000, I had become

7   773 So.2d 7 (Fla. 2000).

concerned that Justice Lewis was unwilling to consider the practical consequences of cases we decided. I had begun to find Justice Lewis increasingly rigid in making decisions and decreasingly open to discussion. Since I believed that it was necessary for our court to understand and consider the practical ramifications of our decisions, and that it was very helpful to have a candid one-on-one conversation with another justice about some cases, Justice Lewis and I often divided as to results and methods in deciding cases. This difference became significant at the end of the presidential election contest case.

The most recently appointed justice was Peggy Quince. She was born in Norfolk, Virginia, and had graduated in 1970 from Howard University in Washington, D.C., with a bachelor's degree in zoology. She received her law degree in 1975 from Catholic University of America, which is also in Washington, D.C. She began her legal career in Washington, D.C., as a hearing officer with the Rental Accommodations Office. Thereafter she moved to Florida and began a civil law practice in Bradenton. In 1980, she began a thirteen-year tenure with the state attorney general handling appeals, concentrating at the end of her service on appeals in death-penalty cases.

In 1993, Justice Quince became the first African American female appointed to the court of appeals by Governor Chiles, who named her to the Supreme Court in 1998, with the agreement of then governor-elect Jeb Bush. Though she had been on our court only a brief time, I had found Justice Quince to be a very capable addition to the court and a pleasant colleague, even though we sometimes did not agree. Justice Quince often voted in cases with Justices Anstead and Pariente.

Though Justices Lewis and Quince most often formed the majority with Justices Shaw, Anstead, and Pariente, both Justice Lewis and Justice Quince joined me in dissenting in the important *Armstrong v. Harris* decision.[8]

These were the lead players in the cast at the Florida Supreme Court, which would receive, review, and decide the presidential election cases.

---

8   773 So.2d 7 (Fla. 2000).

4

The Supporting Cast

The first significant case in the election dispute was not filed in the Florida state courts, but rather in the United States District Court for the Southern District of Florida in Miami. Linda and I heard the news of the filing as we were driving to Gainesville on Friday, November 10, 2000, to participate in the University of Florida homecoming weekend. The case was assigned to and heard by my friend Judge Don Middlebrooks.

Judge Middlebrooks had started his legal career in Orlando. He then became legal counsel to Governor Reubin Askew. I had headed up Askew's group of active supporters in the Orlando area, and worked with Judge Middlebrooks on various issues. I knew him as a friend with an exceptional legal mind and to be extremely diligent and thorough in whatever task with which he was charged. For a fleeting moment I thought to myself, "Yes!! Maybe Good Ol' Don will find a way to keep the case in the federal courts." But, of course, I knew that was wishful (or wistful) thinking. The laws that governed the election were state, not federal, laws. I knew not even my old friend Don Middlebrooks could keep this storm away from our court. By Monday afternoon, November 13, 2000, Judge Middlebrooks had dismissed the Bush action, and the focus turned back to the Florida courts.

Back in Tallahassee on Sunday, after our weekend in Gainesville, I went to the court and finished my preparation for our regularly scheduled Tuesday conference of the justices. After reviewing the conference agenda, I took a closer look at election statutes related to vote-counting deadlines. I was still concerned about the difference between the seven-day deadline that the media was reporting, and the ten-day deadline for the overseas ballots. To my chagrin, this reading revealed several sections that struck me as being in conflict with other sections. In this razor's-edge separation of votes between Bush and Gore, these statutory conflicts were obviously fertile ground for legal disputes. It did not take long for this field to be plowed.

In preparation for the coming disputes, Hunter, my law clerk, gave me several election-related decisions by our court to review. One of those cases was *Beckstrom v. Volusia County*,[1] which I had written in 1998. The *Beckstrom* case dealt with absentee ballots in a county sheriff's election. I had been on the bench four years when that case came before the court. The issue in *Beckstrom* was whether black felt-tip markers used to color in absentee ballots complied with the technical requirements of the election statutes. In the opinion, the court refused to throw out the absentee ballots because of technical noncompliance with the election statute since there was no proof that these black markers affected the results of the election. When writing this opinion, my focus was on a local election. I, of course, had no idea at that time that it would ever have bearing on a presidential election. But reading the *Beckstrom* decision brought home the hard reality that many applicable sections of Florida's election laws did not differentiate between the election of local officers and the election of the president of the United States. The counsel for Gore early in the controversy fastened upon the *Beckstrom* opinion to support the argument that technical compliance with election law deadlines should not take precedence over manually counting ballots that the machines allegedly had failed to count.

That Sunday afternoon I gathered the clerk of the court, Tom Hall; the court's marshal, Wilson Barnes; and the court information officer, Craig Waters, in my office, and the four of us had the first of many conferences concerning administrative requirements involved in processing the election cases. These administrative details were essential to the court's running smoothly and required a team of skilled pros. Fortunately for all participants in the cases that followed, these men

---

1   707 So.2d 720 (Fla. 1998).

and their staffs were exceptionally skilled, competent, and caring pro-
fessionals who expertly processed the details of every case.

Each had extraordinary duties that, if not performed competently,
could have stifled, if not stopped, the processing of the cases. This
would have worsened an already tense and sometimes unwieldy situation. Attorney Tom Hall had been appointed Supreme Court clerk in
1999. He had practiced law in Miami before moving to Tallahassee as
chief law clerk at the First District Court of Appeals, where he had both
substantive law and administrative responsibilities. As the clerk of the
Supreme Court, he had followed Sid White, who had held that position
for decades and had developed an experienced staff.

The clerk's office is the heart of an appellate court's operation. It is
responsible for handling papers that are the sum and substance of every legal proceeding. Papers must be filed, maintained, and presented
to the judges in an orderly and timely way. The loss or misplacement of
a single piece of paper can materially change the decision in a case. During the presidential cases, the number of cases and papers filed in such
a short period that had to be organized and made immediately available
to the justices and their staffs was unprecedented. In 2000, our clerk's
office did not have the benefit of electronic filing nearly to the level that
would be in operation in the clerk's office only a couple of years after
2000. Thus, many papers had to be filed and circulated by hand.

While attending to this unprecedented amount of paperwork, the
clerk's office also had to handle the heavy load of other cases (including
capital cases in which a defendant had been sentenced to death) the
court was processing. To the parties and lawyers involved in these other
cases, their cases were as important as the presidential election. We realized the presidential election cases would make exceptional demands
upon us, but we had to make sure our regular case processing was unaf-
fected. Looking back, I can say without hesitation that my faith in the
clerk's office under Tom Hall's leadership was justified.

Wilson Barnes, the marshal of the Florida Supreme Court for ten
years, was a retired regular U.S. Army lieutenant colonel and another
consummate professional. Friendly and affable, Wilson also had the
demeanor of a colonel. When he spoke, you listened. In Tallahassee,

he worked with the NAACP and Florida A&M University and had an excellent working relationship with the law-enforcement agencies, all of whom we would later call on as large crowds descended upon the Florida Supreme Court. While the daily crowds in front of the Supreme Court Building were politically and emotionally charged, we had orderly crowd control outside the court throughout the thirty-six days. Despite the growing tensions, I received no complaints from anyone who felt that the marshal and his staff did not treat them with courtesy and respect.

Without the professional skills of Craig Waters, the court's information officer, I doubt we could have processed the election cases we heard. An attorney and former newspaperman, he had been a law clerk before becoming the information officer in 1997, and he was uncommonly skilled in writing and using computers. The court was unknown to almost all who were watching, and the first impression about the demeanor and competence of the court was vital. Craig was that first impression. It was no exaggeration when I told others that Craig's periodic appearance on the front steps of the court building was like the "cuckoo coming out of the clock." He made all the announcements about the court's actions and even nonactions, popping out day and night from inside the court to tell the world what was occurring inside.

Craig also handled the numerous requests by news organizations for information. He screened the enormous e-mail onslaught that hit the court's computers. We went from receiving two thousand e-mails a day to two million. He organized the televising of the two oral arguments the court would hear. He also helped select press representatives who were in the court for those arguments. Our court had been one of only a few state supreme courts that had a full-time court information officer. Since the election, however, many other courts have sought Craig's advice on developing those offices.

As I left the court that Sunday afternoon, I noticed that a foreign media group had set up a tent on the front lawn of the court—the first in what would grow into a large tent city. It was soon moved across the street to the steps of the Capitol Building so that the marshal's staff could better manage the ever-increasing crowds. Along the street, trucks with broadcasting equipment began lining up; eventually they would take up approximately three blocks. I called Marshal Barnes and said that it was apparent that we had to get set up to handle the growing number of media and interested citizens. Marshal Barnes and Craig swung into action. By Monday afternoon, they had a plan in place.

5

Florida Election Law

Over the first weekend after the election, the pace escalated in many parts of the state. On Monday morning, November 13, 2000, glancing at Florida newspapers, I read about disorder and confusion concerning votes in Palm Beach, Broward and Miami-Dade Counties. The *Miami Herald* headlined: "The Gap Narrows" with the subtitle, "Gore Moves within a Thousand Votes." The lead front-page article detailed errors in recounts under way in Miami-Dade, Broward, and Pinellas Counties. Pinellas elections officials in Clearwater later retracted their reported election results, ordering another recount.

Dade elections supervisor David Leahy said a likely reason for the newly found votes was hanging chads. Chads are the little paper squares that voters punch through to cast a vote when voting what was known as a "punch-card ballot."[1] Sometimes a chad will hang by a corner instead of detaching and keep the computers from tallying the vote correctly. But in a manual recount, the delicate chads could come off, altering the ballot in a way that the voter did not intend.

Long before the election, I had agreed to speak that Monday to a luncheon meeting of state's attorneys from Florida's twenty court circuits

---

1   Punch-card ballots were used in twenty-four of Florida's sixty-seven counties. To vote these ballots, voters used a stylus to pop chads out of a computer-card Votomatic ballot or a lever machine to punch a hole in paper Datavote ballots. Ballots are tabulated centrally. The counties in which these ballots were used were Broward, Collier, DeSoto, Dixie, Duval, Gilchrist, Glades, Hardee, Highlands, Hillsborough, Indian River, Jefferson, Lee, Madison, Marion, Miami-Dade, Nassau, Osceola, Palm Beach, Pasco, Pinellas, Sarasota, Sumter, and Wakulla (*Orlando Sentinel*, "Exposing the Flaw," November 12, 2001).

who had gathered for their annual meeting. These are the men and women who prosecute criminal cases. The meeting was in Marco Island in southwest Florida. I flew to the meeting in the state-owned plane so I could immediately return to Tallahassee. During the preluncheon social time, there was only limited chatter about the closeness of the election and the chaos spilling out across the state.

I began my comments by saying I was glad to get away from Tallahassee for a little while "because by the end of the week there would be real controversy in the capital." After a pause, I said, "I'm referring to the quarterback controversy . . . who's going to be Florida's starting quarterback?" For an audience packed with graduates of the University of Florida in Gainesville and its cross-state rival in Tallahassee, the Florida State Seminoles, that was the relevant controversy, because at that point in time that issue was more on the minds of most of my audience than were the claims surrounding the presidential election ballots. The Seminoles were hosting their arch-rival the Gators that weekend, and the sports pages were focused on whether Florida coach Steve Spurrier would start Rex Grossman or Jesse Palmer as quarterback. In my remarks to the state's attorneys, I could not, of course, ignore the election altogether, but I confined my comments to nonpolitical aspects. I mentioned, for example, how the media and attorneys and representatives of Bush and Gore were having a tough time finding hotel rooms in Tallahassee. "Football fans booked every room in the area months and months ago." By the end of that week, accommodations had become a real problem.

When I arrived back in my office in Tallahassee late Monday afternoon, Judge Middlebrooks's order was on my desk.[2] I read his ruling, and, as I knew he would, he had written an excellent order that I thought clearly explained a good part of Florida's statutory election scheme. Bush's attorneys had argued that Florida statutes, which allowed a manual recount of votes, would diminish the accuracy of a vote count because of ballot degradation; further, they said county canvassing boards had violated voters' First and Fourteenth Amendment rights by not having their votes counted in an equal and consistent

---

2   *Seigel v. LePore* 120 F. Supp.2nd 1041 (November 13, 2000).

way with all other voters. Bush wanted to stop manual recounting in Volusia, Palm Beach, Broward, and Miami-Dade Counties.

Judge Middlebrooks concluded that Bush had failed to demonstrate that manual recounts were so unreliable that they caused constitutional injury and, importantly for our court's planning, Judge Middlebrooks found no evidence that Bush lacked an adequate remedy in state court for any claim he might otherwise have under the Florida elections statutes. The public interest, he concluded, was best served by denying Bush's federal court petition.

After reading Judge Middlebrooks's order, I studied the complaint filed in a suit involving the vote in Volusia County. The suit had been filed in the Leon County (Tallahassee) Circuit Court seeking an order directing Secretary of State Katherine Harris to extend the time when the county's election results had to be filed with the Department of State. This suit focused on the problem of the statutory seven-day deadline, which had become evident to me when I reviewed the election laws the previous Sunday. Secretary Harris had announced she would enforce the statutory deadline of seven days from the election for all counties, requiring them to forward to the state their certified vote counts in the presidential election. Her deadline for the counties was November 14, 2000—which was the next day!

I knew the time had come for me to examine the election statutes more closely, particularly Sections 102.111 and 102.112, which had previously concerned me. Florida Statute 102.111, titled "Elections Canvassing Commission," said that immediately after the certification of any federal or state election by the county canvassing board, the results shall be forwarded to the Department of State. The governor, the secretary of state, and the director of the Division of Elections (comprising the commission) shall certify the returns of the election and declare a winner. The statute expressly concluded: "If the county's returns are not received by the Department of State by 5:00 p.m. of the seventh day following an election, all missing counties shall be ignored, and the results on file shall be certified."

Florida Statute 102.112, titled "Deadline for Submission of County Returns to the Department of State," obviously also dealt with forwarding election returns from the counties to the Department of State.

Returns were similarly required to be filed by 5:00 p.m. on the seventh day following the election, but this provision expressly stated: "If the returns are not received by the department by the time specified such returns may be ignored and the results on file at that time may be certified by the department." The statute added that the "department shall fine each board member $200 for each day returns are late, to be paid only from the board member's personal funds and deposited into the Election Campaign Financing Trust Fund, created by s.106.32." The plain conflict between these statutory sections was that Section .111 used the words "shall be ignored," which connoted a mandatory enforcement of the sanction, whereas Section .112 used the words "may be ignored," which connoted that the department had discretion in enforcing the sanction. I could find no ready explanation for the use of "shall" in one section and the use of "may" in the other.

As I'd noted earlier, the alarming aspect of the statutes was that whether the word "shall" or the word "may" controlled the present enforcement of the statutes, the time for this certification was only seven days from the date of the election. Considering the large populations and voter turnout in Palm Beach, Broward, and Miami-Dade Counties, where recounts reportedly were ongoing or being considered, seven days was obviously an impossible deadline.

I then examined Florida Statute 102.166, titled "Protest of Election Returns Procedure," and found another contradiction. This statute provided that any qualified candidate or elector could protest the returns as being erroneous by filing a sworn written protest. The protest was permitted to "be filed with the canvassing board prior to the time the canvassing board certified the results for the office being protested or within five days after the midnight of the date the election is held, whichever occurs later." In plain language, that statute meant that a protest could be filed right up to the deadline for filing returns with the Department of State. This left no time for a canvassing board to recount votes—which the canvassing board was directed to do if the board found that the requirements of the protest statute had been demonstrated.

The headline on the front page of the November 13, 2000, *Tampa Tribune* voiced my concern: "Vote Deadline Too Soon for Hand Recount."

According to the *Tribune*, Palm Beach County planned to recount all 462,000 ballots by hand. Time was an obvious problem, and that's not even considering other potential problems involved with manually recounting punch-card ballots.

Another section in the election statute 102.168 also caught my attention. Entitled "Contest of Election," it stated that an unsuccessful candidate or qualified elector can contest certification of an election. Such contests had to be filed in the circuit court "within ten days after midnight of the date the last county canvassing board empowered to canvass the returns certifies the results of the election being contested or five days after midnight of the date the last county canvassing board empowered to canvass the returns certifies the results of that particular election following a protest pursuant to s.102.166, whichever occurs later." This meant an election could not be contested until the last county canvassing board certified the returns in the election. The contest in a statewide election had to be filed in the circuit court of Leon County.

Grounds to contest an election were spelled out very broadly and included "receipt of a number of illegal votes or rejection of a number of legal votes sufficient to change or place in doubt the result of the election"; "any other cause or allegation which, if sustained, would show that a person other than the successful candidate was the person duly nominated or elected to the office in question." The canvassing board or the election board was designated to be the proper defendant in an action brought under the statute. Pursuant to the statute, the circuit judge handling the case had complete authority to investigate, examine, and check into each allegation in the complaint and "to correct any alleged wrong and to provide any relief appropriate under such circumstances." As I read the statutes, I realized that, although the protest process gave power to the county canvassing boards to decide whether to manually recount votes, the legislature had given Florida circuit courts very broad latitude after the protests were completed to correct any election defects. These statutorily authorized contests were going to require time to process.

Two simple but direct questions in this brewing controversy became apparent to me. How long could these protests and contests go on?

If they dragged on too long, was it possible that Florida's electors would not be counted in the presidential Electoral College? These were issues I needed to examine, but given how much was happening, I put them off for another day.

Before I left the court, I called Tom Hall, Marshal Barnes, and Craig Waters to my office for the latest updates from around the state. I learned that the Volusia County case had been assigned to Leon County Circuit Judge Terry Lewis. Tom said that Judge Lewis had scheduled a hearing for 11:00 a.m. the next day, which would be November 14, 2000. The hearing would be six hours before the time at which Secretary Harris announced she would stop accepting county certifications. Tom also said he had received word that another suit had been filed in Palm Beach County, but we did not have the details.

Even for a Monday, this had been a very long day. I went home.

6

Conflicting Opinions

Harris v. Butterworth

As the election cases developed, it became obvious that the officials in charge of both the State Division of Elections and the Florida Office of the Attorney General were handicapped by having had political affiliations with the candidates during the presidential campaign. Secretary of State Katherine Harris had been actively involved in Bush's campaign, and Attorney General Bob Butterworth had been affiliated with the Gore campaign. This made their objectivity suspect, and I did not believe the usual deferential weights should be given to their legal opinions regarding the election statutes. In a usual situation, the legal opinion from the State Division of Elections as to election laws, and the attorney general's legal opinions as to the meaning of all statutes are given great weight by Florida's courts. But this was not the usual situation. Here the legal opinions of these top officials were in conflict, and their opinions favored the candidate that each had backed in the election.

It was the seventh day after the election, and Secretary Harris wasn't backing down. A day earlier she had issued a statement bluntly declaring that she intended to enforce the seven-day deadline for all sixty-seven counties in Florida to file their returns with the state. She specifically instructed the director of the Division of Elections to put the Palm Beach County Canvassing Board on notice that if it didn't comply with the deadline, Palm Beach's votes would not be counted in the election. The Division of Elections issued a legal opinion that the authorization for recounting ballots had to be tied to a defect in voting-machine counts.

On the other side, Attorney General Butterworth issued an advisory legal opinion to Judge Burton, the chairman of the Palm Beach County Canvassing Board, on the same statute dealing with errors in vote tabulations. He concluded that the opinion from the Division of Elections on November 13, 2000, as to the meaning of "error in voting tabulation which could affect the outcome of an election" was wrong.

There was no doubt now that these issues would soon be in our court, but that day we had other important issues on our conference agenda, including one we had been working on since early in the spring of 2000—revising the rules of procedure for capital postconviction proceedings. We stated in our April 2000 opinion declaring the legislature's Death Penalty Reform Act unconstitutional that we would revise postconviction procedural rules for capital cases, and that was what we were working to do. In anticipation of a lengthy court conference, I had asked Major Harding to order lunch from the café at his Episcopal church to be served during the conference.

We began the meeting at the usual 9:00 a.m. and worked our way through the agenda until we took a lunch break. Shortly after we began eating, Tom Hall came into the conference room and announced that Leon County Circuit Court Judge Terry Lewis had denied the petition for an injunction in the action brought by the Volusia County Canvassing Board. The news that the circuit court had not enjoined Secretary Harris clearly upset some of the justices. I noted Barbara Pariente and Peggy Quince were visibly shaken. Others just got up without saying a word and left the conference room for a few minutes. I believe at that time the reality of the magnitude of what our court was going to have to confront struck all of us. We all knew that this case would soon reach us.

Within about fifteen minutes, the justices who had left the conference room returned, and we began our initial focus on what would likely be the process of the case decided by Judge Lewis. Tom Hall did not yet have a copy of Circuit Judge Lewis's order so we did not at that time know its substance, nor did we know the timing of an appeal. A direct appeal of Judge Lewis's decision would go to the First District

Court of Appeals. It was possible that the First District Court could hear and decide the case. But the Florida Constitution provides that in cases certified by a district court to be of great public importance and requiring immediate resolution by the Supreme Court, the district court can pass those cases directly to the Supreme Court. We were confident under the circumstances that the First District would pass along to our court an appeal of Judge Lewis's order. This would be the case that would be the primary basis for our court to resolve the escalating controversy. In deciding the case, we would resolve the conflicting legal opinions of the secretary of state and the attorney general.

This meant that we needed to discuss the schedule for hearing this case. All the justices were concerned about the time problem inherent in the case and the calendar, and all were aware of the time limitations in the state election statutes. We also understood that there was a time limitation for the Electoral College, but were less well informed about that aspect of the law. Another very immediate timing issue was that the Thanksgiving holiday was the following week. We all believed it was important to hear and decide the case before Thanksgiving. We recognized and discussed that the controversy would likely be exacerbated if the appeal lingered over the four-day holiday weekend without a decision from us.

Hearing oral arguments in a case on the Friday after Thanksgiving, and issuing an opinion over the weekend presented logistical difficulties for all parties involved—the lawyers, the court, and the staff. We therefore concluded that, although it would be difficult to hear oral arguments on Monday, November 20, 2000, which was less than a week away, and considering that we didn't even yet have the case in our court, we had no real alternative. This would give us just a day or so to deliberate and issue an opinion before Thanksgiving.

Fortunately, we had considerable experience deciding cases under time pressure. Every time the governor signed a death warrant, we were forced to consider last-minute appeals filed on behalf of condemned prisoners, often having to schedule and have oral argument in less than a week. Therefore, once we committed to this schedule, we began to plan accordingly.

When the news of Circuit Judge Lewis's ruling spread, the public gaze turned to our court, and the crowd outside the Supreme Court, which had been building steadily, grew even larger. The crowd was beginning to take the form of both a demonstration and a carnival. Clowns, jugglers, and other acts performed before the crowd, and they took place right below the chief's conference room, where we were having lunch. I distinctly remember a lady who brought a skunk that she had taught to do tricks. While the acts were intended to express the view that what was going on inside the building was a circus, the acts did not cause any problems and, in fact, entertained the crowd, which was not a bad thing.

Across Duval Street from where the crowd had gathered, media broadcasting trucks, with equipment atop the roofs, could be seen lining the street. On the steps of the Capitol, directly across the street from the Supreme Court Building, the media had created a tent city that probably had forty to fifty tents. All of this reinforced in our minds the conviction that we had to decide this matter quickly and rule before Thanksgiving.

That afternoon, when I returned to my office, Tom Hall came in and advised me that he had been notified that the Palm Beach Canvassing Board, in a separate case filed originally in our court, was going to ask our court to resolve the conflicting legal opinions that it had received from Secretary Harris and Attorney General Butterworth. Tom also advised me that Secretary Harris's lawyers intended to file an action in our court. It was apparent that these actions might not arrive by the regular 5:00 p.m. closing time for the clerk's office. Since it appeared that the filings were imminent, I told Tom to keep staff available to receive the filings.

As it turned out, the filings did not arrive until around 3:00 a.m. on November 15, 2000. After that, I advised Tom to have the clerk's office open at regular hours unless we had a clear necessity to do otherwise. We were able in most instances to keep to this rule, except for receiving briefs during the weekend and on Thanksgiving Day when there was an emergency filing to restart the vote recount in Miami-Dade.

At the conference, other than discussing the scheduling issues, we did not discuss any of the details of the presidential election cases. But I read into what was said and the participants' facial expressions that the justices were surprised that Circuit Judge Lewis had denied the petition and were eager to see the order he had entered.

When I got to my office, Circuit Judge Lewis's order was on my desk:

> The heart of the issue raised by the Motion is this: Section 102.166, Florida Statutes, contemplates that upon request a county canvassing board may authorize a manual recount of votes cast in an election. Both Volusia and Palm Beach Counties have so authorized, and are in the process of conducting, a manual recount. The Boards are concerned that the manual recounts may not be completed by 5 p.m., today, November 14, 2000, which is the deadline imposed upon them by Section 102.112, Florida Statutes, to certify and report the election returns to the Secretary of State. This section provides that if the returns are not received by the deadline, such returns may be ignored by the Secretary of State in her certification of results statewide.

> The plaintiffs insist that the Secretary of State must consider the certified results from Volusia and Palm Beach Counties, even if they are filed late, if they are still engaged in the manual recount of the votes. The Secretary of State insists that, absent an Act of God such as a hurricane, any returns not received by the statutory deadline will not be counted in the statewide tabulations and certification of the election results. For the reasons set forth below, I find that the County Canvassing Boards must certify and file what election returns they have by the statutory deadline of 5:00 p.m. of November 14, 2000, with due notification to the Secretary of State of any pending manual recount, and may thereafter file supplemental or corrective returns. The Secretary of State may ignore such late returns, but may not do so arbitrarily, rather, only by the proper exercise of discretion after consideration of all appropriate facts and circumstances.

> Just as the Secretary cannot decide ahead of time what late returns should or should not be ignored, it would not be proper for me to do so by injunction. I can lawfully direct the Secretary

to properly exercise her discretion in making a decision on the returns, but I cannot enjoin the Secretary to make a particular decision, nor can I rewrite the Statute which, by its plain meaning, mandates the filing of returns by the Canvassing Boards by 5:00 p.m. on November 14, 2000.

I thought the order set out a reasoned analysis of the issues and statutes in the case, and reached what appeared to me to be a reasonable middle ground. The order held that the counties had to comply with the 5:00 p.m., November 14, 2000, deadline, but that the counties could later file supplementary or corrective returns and the secretary of state could not ignore the supplementary or corrective returns arbitrarily.

I thought Judge Lewis's ruling was a good first step. I then learned that Secretary Harris had reacted to Judge Lewis's order by announcing that she would expect certified returns from all sixty-seven counties by the statutory deadline and setting a deadline of 2:00 p.m. on November 15, 2000, for counties to justify revisions to the certifications. I knew that her announcement would only add fuel to the fire.

I headed home, hoping to get a good night's rest and wondering what twists and turns the next day would hold.

7

Petitions in Our Court

The two original actions filed over the night of November 14 and 15 were not ordinary filings in the Florida Supreme Court because the cases had not been originally filed in a lower court. An original filing of a case in the Supreme Court is an extraordinary action since, with few exceptions, cases are accepted at the Florida Supreme Court only after being reviewed and decided by the Florida lower courts.

The Palm Beach County Canvassing Board's petition sought resolution of the conflicting legal opinions of the secretary of state and the attorney general. I questioned in my mind whether the action was properly within the Supreme Court's jurisdiction as an original action. In the other original action, Secretary Harris sought to temporarily suspend the manual vote recounts in those counties until there was a decision whether election results certified earlier could be modified. The action also sought to have all the litigation from the various counties transferred to Leon County. Secretary Harris's petition was a broad statement of complications in various cases, which had been filed throughout the state. In reading the petition, I did not see a basis under the Florida Constitution for such an original action in our court. It was essentially a plea to stop the growing quagmire of litigation in multiple counties. While this appealed to me to protect the Florida court system from being overwhelmed by the sheer volume of cases that were being filed, the narrow jurisdiction given to the Supreme Court by the Florida Constitution did not provide a basis to accept and decide such a case filed originally in our court.

I scheduled a conference at 2:00 p.m. on November 15, 2000, to consider the two petitions. I was eager to hear the other justices' views.

I next met with Craig Waters, who arranged for the executive director of the Florida Broadcasters Association to come to my office to discuss arrangements for the television broadcast of the oral argument on November 20, 2000. During this meeting, we worked out an arrangement by which there would be only one live feed from the courtroom that could be broadcast by all the networks that wanted to carry the oral argument live. This would eliminate video cameras in the courtroom, since we could do this with the equipment that was used for all of our oral arguments. This equipment used portals near the ceiling of the courtroom and did not interfere with the proceedings at all.

Our court conference began promptly at 2:00 p.m. and lasted almost three hours. Following exhaustive (and exhausting) discussion, the court decided to deny the Harris petition, concluding, as I had when I first read it, that it was not an original action that came within the court's jurisdiction. The longer discussion was about the Palm Beach County Canvassing Board's original action. While all the justices recognized that this was really not a proper original action filed in our court, a majority of the justices believed that, in view of the severe time limitations involved, a resolution of the conflicting opinions issued by the secretary of state and the attorney general was needed. I certainly agreed with this practical assessment. Following long discussion, the court finally unanimously agreed to order the secretary of state, the attorney general, and other interested parties to file a response to the canvassing board's petition by the next day. This action would give our court the benefit of the lawyers' arguments as to whether the court had jurisdiction to decide the controversy involving the conflicting opinions.

I had substantial reservations about not ruling the same way on both petitions. I favored ordering a response to Secretary Harris's petition as well or dismissing the canvassing board's petition, but making it clear in the order dismissing the petition that the issues raised by the canvassing board would be considered in the appeal we were going to review in the case decided by Circuit Judge Lewis. The canvassing board had already joined in the appeal in that case. I was concerned that the media and the interested parties would read the denial of the Harris petition and the ordering of a response to the canvassing board's petition as a decision that favored the Gore side. But others did not agree. Others believed that Secretary Harris's petition was completely bereft of a jurisdictional basis and that there was no compelling reason not to recognize that fact. Since I agreed with them that Secretary Harris's petition was not a proper original action, in the end I went along with dismissing that petition.

No sooner had our conference ended than I learned that Secretary Harris had rejected appeals by officials in Palm Beach, Broward, Miami-Dade, and Collier Counties to revise certified returns filed earlier. The secretary said that the reasons provided for counting after the seven-day deadline had failed to demonstrate proof of voter fraud that affected the outcome of the election; or reasonable doubt that the certified results expressed the will of the voters; or that elected officials were prevented from complying with deadlines as a result of an act of God or extenuating circumstances beyond their control, such as an electrical power outage.

Further, in establishing the standards for her decision, she noted that there had to be "more than a mere possibility that the outcome of the election would have been affected." According to Secretary Harris, where there had been substantial compliance with statutory election procedures and the contested results related to voter error, there continued to be a reasonable expectation that the certified results expressed the will of the voters.

Secretary Harris had also issued a statement announcing that the State Election Commission had certified the results of the presidential election except for the overseas ballots.[1] She went on to note that the overseas ballots would be completed on Saturday, November 18, 2000, and that the winner of the presidential election would be finally certified at that time. Secretary Harris's announcement ended with a statement that "the schedule, of course, is subject to judicial intervention."

---

1   See chapter 2, note 1.

Secretary Harris's statement denying the amended returns was issued soon after Craig Waters published our order denying Harris's petition. On my way home, I heard a radio news report that the Florida Supreme Court had ordered that the manual counting continue. Actually, we had not issued such an order, but I understood how our ruling could have been interpreted that way. By dismissing Harris's petition to stop manual recounts in those four counties, we had given the canvassing boards the green light to keep recounting.

8

Tension Mounts

As I anticipated, an anti-Harris bias was ascribed by the news media to our decision to deny the Harris petition and to order a response to the Palm Beach Canvassing Board's petition. I had hoped the court's action would be perceived as more neutral as the election results headed for oral argument in our court. Instead, our order was seen as supporting Gore and reprimanding Harris.

I was keenly aware, of course, that the members of our court had all been appointed by Democratic governors, and that all of the justices, with the exception of Major Harding, were registered Democrats and thus the court was portrayed by the news media as having a built-in bias favoring Gore.[1] I did not believe that this superficial assessment accurately explained the predilections of the justices. It certainly did not explain my thought processes. The facts of the appointments and party registrations in and of themselves did not result in the justices being biased in favor of Gore. It is my experience that once a person is appointed to a court of last resort, which the Florida Supreme Court is, that person views him- or herself as being a political free agent, just as I did.

I hasten to add, however, that I am not maintaining that the justices were not predisposed toward one or the other of the candidates. Being a political free agent means that a justice can and does make decisions based upon his or her own personal philosophies. As I previously

---

1   Dana Summer's cartoon in the *Orlando Sentinel*, November 26, 2000, depicted the Florida Supreme Court justices as the "Committee to Elect Al Gore."

explained, five members of our court were philosophically liberal. Gore was the more liberal of the two candidates; therefore, it was my conclusion at the time that the leanings of the majority of the justices were in favor of Gore. Yet at this stage of the controversy, and actually through the end of the protest phase, I did not perceive that the decisions made by our court were the result of predisposed leanings in favor of Gore.

By midmorning on November 16, 2000, we received the response to the canvassing board petition we had ordered. I had been scheduled to be in Pensacola to discuss budgeting for the state court system, but I canceled that trip and sent word to the justices that we would gather in the downstairs conference room to discuss the Palm Beach Canvassing Board's petition. We had a long debate about the petition and ultimately deferred a decision on whether we had jurisdiction to decide the petition. All of us recognized the slender jurisdictional reed supporting the argument for the case to be an original action in our court. The case should have been originally filed in the circuit court and proceeded to our court through the district court, as the case before Circuit Judge Lewis had. There was a general view among the justices, however, that the opinion issued by the secretary of state as to the recounts was in all likelihood wrong, and that her erroneous opinion had resulted in the loss of valuable time in the recounting of the ballots in accord with the statutory procedure that appeared to authorize manual recounts. Therefore, we did not want to dismiss the petition out of concern that such a dismissal would be interpreted in a way that would result in further loss of time in the recounting. Rather, we all concluded that we should defer a decision as to the conflicting opinions of the secretary of state and the attorney general. We knew we would deal with that conflict in reviewing the case decided by Circuit Judge Lewis.

In our conference discussion we knew that the circuit court in Palm Beach County had ruled the canvassing board could complete a manual recount. We did not want any order we entered to be read as a contrary decision. For this reason we agreed to enter an order that stated:

We enter the present interim order on this matter. We have considered the petition and it appears that the relief sought on the question of whether the canvassing board may conduct a manual recount of the votes cast for president and vice president has been answered in the affirmative in the circuit courts of Leon and Palm Beach counties. At present this is binding legal authority to the recounts continuing and there is no legal impediment to the recounts continuing. Thus, petitioners are authorized to proceed with the manual recount.

I was in favor of this order because I wanted to clarify that we intended for the time between the present and the date we ruled in Circuit Judge Lewis's case not to be wasted. If the manual counting ceased on the date we issued the above order, a later decision by our court, after considering the merits of the case decided by Judge Lewis, in which we authorized manual counting would come too late to effectively restart the counting, and complete that counting within a reasonable extended time period.

On the other hand, if our court ultimately decided manual recounts were not properly authorized, no harm would result because the manually recounted votes would not be allowed in the vote count. Further, if our court decided votes should not be accepted after the deadline passed, and a federal court ruled we erred in that decision, the revisions could be allowed because the recounts had been completed.

It had long been my view, based upon my work as a trial lawyer, that a record should be developed that is as complete as practical, and that while a case is on appeal, the status quo of the case in controversy should be maintained. That way, an appellate court can make a substantive decision that is not rendered moot by the time involved in studying and deciding the issues. I thought that our order stating there was no reason to stop manual recounting served these purposes. When Craig released the order, the press reported that we had ruled that the manual recounts were to continue.

We actually did not make such an affirmative ruling, though I could certainly understand that interpretation of our ruling. Unfortunately, this interpretation led the media again to widely comment that we had a Gore bias. This concerned me because I knew that a widespread assumption of bias for one side or the other would substantially adversely impact the court's credibility as the decision maker, and at this point I had to assume that our court was going to be the ultimate decision maker in the presidential election controversy.

I was very aware that day that there was a lot of court activity at various judicial levels. The circuit courts in Palm Beach and Broward Counties heard arguments on diverse presidential election issues including the butterfly ballot. There were cases being heard on various presidential election issues in the Florida state courts from the Panhandle counties to the northeastern, central, and southwestern parts of the state. Issues were being considered about absentee ballots in Martin County (north of Palm Beach) and Seminole County (north of Orlando).[2] Rulings in those cases could also have had serious effect on the outcome of the election because so few votes separated Bush and Gore. There was also action in the Eleventh Circuit U.S. Court of Appeals. It had agreed to hear Bush's appeal from Judge Middlebrooks's order denying the petition to stop the manual recounts.

My apprehension about these election cases dominating the work of the state's judicial system was proving justified. Regardless of the significance of the presidential election litigation, the other work of the Florida judicial system had to be heard and acted upon during this period. In our state's courts there were crucial cases involving child custody, juvenile detention, criminal cases where there were speedy trial requirements, and civil cases in which citizens were in need of immediate decisions. The effect on real people in every county in Florida of timely resolution of the daily work in the state courts cannot be overstated, and could not be overlooked. I repeatedly asked Tom Hall, Craig Waters, and the State Office of Court Administration to reiterate to lower courts throughout the state my determination that the usual work of the courts continue regardless of the time pressures of cases involving the presidential election.

Still, our court's central focus was the case being decided by Judge Lewis only two blocks from our building. It was in that case that the

---

2   See *Taylor v. Martin County Canvassing Board* 773 So.2d 517 (Fla. 2000); and *Jacobs v. Seminole County Canvassing Board* 773 So.2d 519 (Fla. 2000).

Gore team petitioned Judge Lewis to declare that Secretary Harris's certification of the election results was null and void, and that we would confront directly the issue of the certification of the winner of the Florida electoral votes.

When our long judicial conference on November 16, 2000, finally ended, I went upstairs to my office. My staff was deep into legal research. It was becoming increasingly apparent from media reports that the central issue in the dispute over manual counting was the use of punch-card ballots. My law clerks' research and the research of staff lawyers for other justices revealed that several states reported litigation involving chads, which were alternately labeled as "hanging chads," "dimpled chads," "swinging chads," "tri chads," and "pregnant chads." It became apparent that problems with punch-card ballots predated Florida's presidential election, and yet the ballots had been widely used in Florida counties including the three—Palm Beach, Broward, and Miami-Dade—in which Gore had filed statutory protests.

After reviewing the research about the punch-card ballots, I headed home. Driving home, I heard public radio report our order on recounts, and also report about the argument before Judge Lewis. The contention now being argued to Judge Lewis was that Secretary Harris had violated his order on revised returns. Judge Lewis was to rule on the Gore motion on November 17, 2000.

The Florida Supreme Court in oral argument.

The dissenters.
Top to bottom:
Charley Wells,
Lee Shaw, and
Major Harding.

The majority. Harry Anstead (*top left*), Fred Lewis (*top right*), Peggy Quince (*middle*), and Barbara Pariente (*bottom*).

Left to right: Wilson Barnes, marshal; Tom Hall, clerk of court; Craig Waters, court information officer.

Charley Wells in chambers during the weekend of November 18, 2000.

Lee Shaw in chambers during the weekend of November 18, 2000.

Major Harding in chambers during the weekend of November 18, 2000.

David Boies, attorney for Al Gore.

Barry Richard, attorney for George W. Bush.

Courtroom during oral argument on November 20, 2000. *Far left*: former U.S. secretary of state, James Baker.

Outside the court on November 17, 2000.

Clerk of Court Tom Hall with the Dade County ballots on December 10, 2000.

Craig Waters announcing court action.

Charley Wells and Lee Shaw (*left*) during oral argument on December 7, 2000.

Media interviews outside of court.

Reverend Jesse Jackson and Congressman Charlie Rangel march to the Florida Supreme Court Building.

Former U.S. Secretary of State Warren Christopher and retired judge Tom Barkdull at oral argument.

9

The Day before a Long Weekend

Tallahassee was alive with excitement about both the upcoming oral argument and the Florida–Florida State game. Nevertheless, everything was calm when I arrived at the court at 6:45 a.m. on November 17, 2000. I found some of my staff already on the job, aware we would be working all weekend researching anticipated legal issues. I did not note any other justices' vehicles in the parking garage when I arrived. However, I knew that it was the habit of Justices Pariente and Quince to work late into the evening, which I had no doubt they had done on the evening of November 16, 2000. I knew that most of the justices' staffs were also hard at work that morning.

I met with Tom Hall, Craig Waters, and Marshal Barnes early that morning to work out administrative details for the oral argument. There was the technical matter that the case had not yet been passed through to us by the district court, but Tom Hall had confirmed with the clerk of the district court that the pass-through would be expedited that day.

Marshal Barnes was working on crowd control with the Highway Patrol and the Florida Department of Law Enforcement. The court had received a number of threats by e-mail and phone. The marshal asked the Highway Patrol to park patrol vehicles in the entrances to the underground garages in order to prevent someone from forcing entry through the garage. Marshal Barnes also requested officers to patrol the halls while the justices were at the court in case there was any breach of security.

At 2:00 p.m., we went into conference to iron out procedures for the weekend. As we began, Tom Hall notified us that the First District had just entered the order passing the appeal of Circuit Judge Lewis's decision to us. Finally, we could set a briefing schedule for opposing counsel to file briefs. We needed an extremely abbreviated schedule to allow us time to study and digest the briefs before hearing oral arguments. We therefore ordered the canvassing boards and Vice President Gore to file briefs by noon on Saturday. Secretary Harris and Governor Bush were to file answer briefs by 9:00 a.m. on Sunday, with the reply briefs by the canvassing boards and Gore to be filed by noon on Sunday. We realized that these were excruciatingly short periods for attorneys to write and edit briefs, but we had no choice.

We then had a discussion of Secretary Harris's announcement that she was going to certify the winner of the election after the overseas ballots were counted on Saturday. Her decision posed another problem in maintaining the status quo until we had an opportunity to consider and rule upon the case. We, however, had a serious technical problem about doing anything about this because Judge Lewis's case had been passed through to our court without any party requesting our court to stay Harris's certification. Usually if there is to be a stay pending review, a party requests that a stay be ordered either in the lower court or in our court.

By this time, it was getting late on Friday afternoon. Without any prolonged discussion, all the justices were of the view that we had to maintain the status quo until we heard and decided the case before us. Thus, even though it was unusual for the court to enter a stay without a request from a party, we unanimously agreed that a stay should be entered to preserve the status quo. We issued the following order:

> In order to maintain the status quo, the Court, on its own motion enjoins the Respondent, Secretary of State and the Respondent Election Canvassing Commission, from certifying the results of the November 7, 2000, presidential election, until further notice of this Court. It is NOT the intent of this Order to stop the counting and conveying to the Secretary of State the results of absentee ballots or any other ballots.

To emphasize that the manual counting should continue while we considered the case, the word "not" was capitalized to read "NOT." I did not favor drafting the order so that "NOT" was capitalized, but I did not feel strongly enough about this point to dissent. In retrospect, I think that emphasis was a mistake, because it became more fodder for the media and the view that our court was biased in favor of Vice President Gore.

In agreeing to this order, I felt that the stopping and starting of manual recounts was confusing. Palm Beach, Broward, and Miami-Dade Counties' canvassing boards stopped and started manual recounts several times. For the whole preceding week, the canvassing boards had had to figure out how to deal with conflicting legal opinions from the State Division of Elections and the attorney general and with different orders from trial judges in the various circuit courts. I was aware that Miami-Dade's canvassing board voted 2–1 not to manually recount and then reversed itself and voted 2–1 to manually count ballots. I thought it was important that we make clear, plainly and repeatedly, that we were not making a decision in the order issued at that time that would change the status quo in the affected counties.

After we agreed to the order, our conference adjourned, not to gather again until the oral argument on Monday, November 20, 2000. It was nine days after the election, and our court had not yet dealt with any substantive issues in the cases. We had conferences daily but only on procedural matters. Every day Craig Waters appeared on the steps of the court building and read our orders dealing with these procedural matters. The Gore and Bush campaigns, the media, and the public, all hungry for fresh details about the litigation, assessed how they thought our court was leaning on substantive issues on the basis of how we decided procedural matters. That was to be expected.

10

The Briefs

Finally, we were into THE weekend, time for the Florida–Florida State football game. As I had known it would, the game attracted even greater crowds to Tallahassee. A sign reading "Bobby Bowden for President" appeared outside the court on Friday afternoon.[1]

Normally this would be a socially packed weekend for Linda and me. Traditionally, Florida State president "Sandy" D'Alemberte invited all of the justices—even those of us who were die-hard Florida Gator fans—to the president's box for the Florida–Florida State game. The guests in the box usually included all of Florida's political leaders including the governor, the elected cabinet officers (including the secretary of state), and leaders from the legislature. I decided early in the week that it would be wiser for Linda and me not to attend this year. I knew that everyone would be respectful of the sensitivity of the situation and not talk in my presence about the election litigation, but it would be awkward. Not going turned out to be a fortuitous decision since our beloved Florida Gators were beaten soundly 30–7.

Despite the game, my attention that Saturday was not on social activities or football. I arrived at the court around 6:00 a.m. We were now literally hours from the most momentous oral argument in the history of the Florida Supreme Court, and probably of any state supreme court in our nation's history. Compounding the pressure of the historical importance was the fact that the oral argument was to be broadcast live,

---

1   Bobby Bowden was the longtime football coach of the Florida State Seminoles.

and would be viewed, scrutinized, and evaluated by people throughout the United States and the world. It was vital for many reasons that all the members of the court be well prepared.

The enormity of the public event came increasingly into focus, but so did the complexity of the legal issues and the time limitations. The unrelenting calendar demanded a decision no later than Tuesday. I realized that the calendar threatened the votes of Florida's electors when the Electoral College gathered in December to cast ballots for president.

I was aware of what was being reported in the newspapers and on television. That had to be only background information. My concentration had to be on what the lawyers presented in their briefs, and what my staff, the other justices' staffs, and I personally developed through our own research.

In this respect, the case was like every other case. I did not, nor did any other justice, parachute in from another planet with no knowledge of what the case was about. Still, we had to be sufficiently disciplined to be guided not by news reports or commentary, but by the lawyers, legal precedent, the law, and the U.S. and Florida Constitutions. As always, we would be influenced by our own life experiences, background, training, logic, and, hopefully, common sense.

I began my work that morning with the understanding that Gore was pushing hard for manual recounts because he was behind in the count and the recounts were his lifeline. I also recognized that he was pursuing recounts only in Palm Beach, Broward, and Miami-Dade Counties because it was from those counties that he had the best chance to pick up sufficient votes to overcome his deficit. I saw absolutely nothing wrong with what Gore was doing. To the contrary, I thought it was a sound strategy. I thought if Bush wanted counts in other counties or statewide, then it was up to Bush to request the recounts in compliance with the statutory requirements and time limits. Obviously, Bush did not want the recounts because he was ahead. It was no mystery that Bush's argument would be that the statutes had to be applied so that the counting ended. There was no sin in either position. Surprisingly, the lawyers for both sides argued that there was something sinister about the other's strategy, which I felt conveyed the impression that the justices were incredibly naïve.

Soon after I arrived in my office, John Keyser walked in. John was a longtime career staff attorney who was then working for Justice Shaw. I had asked him to come in to talk about the case. John and I often did not agree on the outcome of cases, but I respected his experienced analysis and usually found he could help me sort out issues that were within his experience during his long service to the court. Though some justices did not want their staff talking with other justices about cases (something I never really understood or agreed with), Justice Shaw and I had an excellent working relationship, and he never was reluctant for me to pick John's brain and benefit from John's experience.

The discussion with John was very helpful to me because it focused my study upon the key to a decision in the case, which was construing the election statutes. As I had become aware when I studied the Florida election statutes on that first Sunday afternoon after November 7, 2000, the statutes had embedded conflicts that required resolving through statutory construction.

Statutory construction is the regular fare of appellate courts. It is done in case after case, month after month. It is a straightforward and essential judicial function in both our federal and state governments, with powers separated among the legislative, executive, and judicial branches. The concept is elementary. When the legislature passes a statute, and it begins to be implemented and enforced, disputes arise as to what the language of the statute means when it is applied.

The first rule of statutory construction is noncontroversial. That rule is that a statute is to be given the meaning intended by the legislature in adopting the statute. If the language used in the statute is plain, and without conflict when applied, then a statute can simply be given the literal meaning of the words in the statute. However, cases in which a court construes statutes are often controversial because legislative language is either unclear and disputed on its face, because the statute conflicts with other statutes, or because doubt as to the statute's meaning is created by the circumstances in which the statute is applied. This results in courts having to make judgments as to the meaning of the statutes.

Even when language is unclear and disputed, courts should continue to determine the intent of the legislature in adopting the statute.

However, determining that intent from legislative records or statements made by legislators in adopting legislation is often unreliable and speculative. Individual legislators vote on legislation for various reasons, which may or may not reveal what is intended by the statute. Other methods for statutory construction have to be used.

Because this is the routine work of courts, commonly accepted rules of statutory construction to determine legislative intent have developed. The widely accepted rules of statutory construction follow (in descending order of importance):

1. A specific statute controls a general statute.
2. A more recently enacted statute controls an older statute on the same matter.
3. A statute will not be construed in such a way as to make any other statute meaningless or absurd.
4. Related statutory provisions must be read as a whole.

When a member of a political branch of the government (legislative or executive) does not agree with a court's construction of a statute, the legislator or executive will often maintain that the court's decision was merely an implementation of the philosophy of the judge, rather than an application of the language of a statute. Such criticisms are natural and understandable, and are often controversial and emotional responses to politically contentious issues.

As noted, it was apparent from my first reading that the Florida election statutes were ambiguous and had to be construed. The statutes expressly conflicted with each other in the following manner.

Subsection 102.111, which said that if county returns are not received by the secretary of state by 5:00 p.m. of the seventh day following an election, all missing counties "shall be ignored," conflicted with Subsection 102.112, which said that if the returns were not received by 5:00 p.m. of the seventh day following an election, the missing counties "may be ignored." "Shall" is a word of command, while the word "may" connotes discretion. If .111 controlled, then the secretary of state's office had no discretion: the seven-day deadline was mandatory and had to be enforced. If .112 controlled, then the secretary of state's office had discretion. If an administrator such as the secretary of state has discretion, then that discretion has to be exercised reasonably, not arbitrarily.

Another statute that had to be construed was Section 102.166, and it had to be construed in conjunction with .111 and .112. This was the protest statute. The issue in this statute was that it authorized the county canvassing boards to allow manual recounts, and provided that the deadline for any candidate or voter in an election to request and be allowed a manual recount went right up to the seven-day deadline of Subsections .111 and .112. This put the rights in respect to a recount in direct conflict with the deadline, because it would be impossible to meet the deadline and also allow a manual recount right up until the deadline. As a practical matter, manual recounts of all votes in the populous counties of Palm Beach, Broward, and Miami-Dade would take a substantial part, if not all, of the seven days. This statutory disconnect had to be dealt with in order for there to be a resolution to the controversy. I tried to apply the commonly accepted rules of statutory construction to these conflicts in the statutes, but I didn't see how these rules of statutory construction would completely resolve the conflict. Making sense out of these statutes as an overall statutory scheme would require some judgment calls by the court. I had no doubt these calls would turn out to be controversial and evoke emotional responses.

As I had become aware earlier, it was obvious that the issues in Palm Beach, Broward, and Miami-Dade Counties arose from the use of a specific type of ballot called the "punch-card ballot."[2] This ballot gave rise to common complaints in these populous counties. The claims centered upon what had been labeled "chads," which were the various configurations of incomplete punches of the punch cards, which the vote-counting machines did not record as votes for a candidate. Uncounted votes with chads were referred to as "undervotes." Undervotes were ballots in which votes for candidates for other offices could be read from the ballots by the counting machines, but the vote for president was not read. This meant the ballot "undervoted" the election for president. There were also some ballots in which the counting machines read two votes for president, and these ballots were referred

---

2   See chapter 5, note 1.

to as "overvotes." Of course, there could be other reasons than chads for a ballot to vote for offices other than president, but not cast a ballot for president. However, it was considered unlikely that a voter would vote for other offices and not for president. The problem with chads resulting in undervoted ballots became the fundamental basis for the claim that manual counting was needed.

After John departed, I looked at a memo prepared by my staff attorneys concerning the time period for overseas ballots. The memo confirmed that no statutory basis existed for the widely reported ten-day postelection deadline within which overseas ballots had to be received. Rather, this ten-day period was a result of an agreement the State of Florida had entered into with the United States Department of Justice in the early 1980s over a dispute concerning ballots cast overseas, primarily by members of the armed services, and whether they had sufficient time to get these votes to the offices of county supervisors of elections so that the votes would be counted. Although the agreement had not been adopted in the Florida Statutes, there was a provision in the Florida Administrative Code that authorized the ten-day period.

In thinking about this ten-day period, it struck me that it was inconsistent for Secretary Harris to maintain that she had to ignore votes from counties that did not meet the seven-day deadline of Subsection .111, but would accept these overseas ballots if they came in within the ten days. Yet, that is precisely what she announced would happen.

I next read a memorandum prepared by my staff concerning the history of the election laws. Understanding the context of when statutes came into being and the historical circumstances existing at that time is often helpful in understanding legislative intent in adopting the statutes. The origins of the statutory scheme for Florida's elections dated back to the 1800s, although some of the statutes were revised or came into existence much later. The seven-day deadline for filing returns with the State Election Commission was adopted in 1951. However, no records were located that explained why the period was seven days or why Subsection .111 mandated that if the seven-day period was not met, votes "shall be ignored."

Subsection .112 was more recent, having been adopted in 1989. No explanation was found as to why the legislature used the language "may be ignored," or why, when using "may," the legislature left the word "shall" in Subsection .111. Nor was there any explanation found as to how the seven-day deadline was to coordinate with the statutory authorization for requesting and granting countywide manual recounts of votes. This history, then, did not prove to be very enlightening. However, if the more recently enacted statute was to take precedence over the earlier enacted statute, as was the accepted rule of statutory construction, then the "may" of Subsection .112 would prevail over the "shall" of Subsection .111. This would be an objective reason for our construction of the statute, and was important because it then followed that Secretary Harris did have discretion with respect to the seven-day deadline. Again, when an administrator has discretion, it is fundamental that such discretion be reasonably and not arbitrarily exercised. This was what Circuit Judge Lewis had ruled in the case to be argued before our court on Monday.

I next turned to the federal law concerning the counting of electoral votes. The Florida election statutes obviously had to coordinate with federal law. My staff attorneys had again prepared an excellent memo. In Article II of the U.S. Constitution, Congress was authorized to determine the time of choosing presidential electors and the day that the electors were to cast their votes. In conformity with this constitutional authority, Congress had set December 18 as that time. The federal law also provided that each state was authorized to settle any controversies in the state concerning presidential electors, and that the state's resolution would be conclusive if the controversies were finally resolved six days before the date designated for the electors to cast their ballots.

I understood this to mean that all of the controversies concerning the Florida presidential election had to be "finally resolved" by December 12, 2000, if Florida was going to take advantage of this provision that allowed all of the election controversies involving Florida's presidential electors to be conclusively resolved by Florida. This was a "safe-harbor" provision. I further understood that this meant that, if the controversies were not "finally resolved" by December 12, 2000, any dispute about Florida electors would be decided by Congress, and ultimately by the U.S. Supreme Court.

It was readily apparent to me that it was important to Florida citizens that this safe harbor be protected. A failure to meet this safe-harbor deadline would prolong the election controversy and result in Florida's voters losing control over the state's electoral votes. This would lead to an uncharted path that I thought could and would have enormous complications. In my view, lengthy uncertainty in this matter would be fraught with dangerous perils not only for Florida, but for the nation and the world.

Thinking through the federal timeline heightened my focus on the real dilemma of the decision we had to make. Plainly, some of the key issues in the case were garden-variety statutory-construction issues to which we could apply the commonly accepted rules of statutory construction. However, if we resolved the conflict in the statutes to allow more time for manually counting votes, the following questions would naturally follow: (1) How long would the time be extended?; (2) Would the court decide a new time limit?; (3) On what basis would the new time limit be determined? The resolution of these issues was not susceptible to mere application of statutory construction because there was no statutory language to construe.

Additionally, the reality was that all of the time and energy that had been expended since the day of the election dealt with the provisions of the statute pertaining to protests. The controversy had to date been directed at the county canvassing boards. Yet, the statutes were clear that upon completion of this phase of the process, the candidates and voters would still be able to *contest the election* by seeking relief in a circuit court. That phase would be equally, if not more, controversial, and potentially more important than the protests. The statute authorized the circuit court to investigate the election and provide appropriate relief. This remedy was, in fact, more comprehensive than the remedy provided in the protests. Whatever we did in our decision following the oral argument on Monday, the contest phase would begin shortly thereafter. To get to finality, the contests would also have to proceed through final appeal.

This would require time, and if the safe-harbor provision was to be protected, time was quickly diminishing. In football parlance, I came to the conclusion that we were only approaching half-time, not the end of the game, and that, if the protest phase was prolonged, we would reduce the time for the contests to be considered in the second half. Under the statutes, the "contest" phase could not begin until the protest phase ended.

With this background and understanding now clear to me, I began studying the papers filed by the lawyers representing the various parties. I knew many of these lawyers through professional and social activities over the years. Those whom I did not know personally I knew by reputation.

Bruce Rogow, representing the Palm Beach Canvassing Board, was a former law-school classmate. He had for many years been a professor at Nova University College of Law in Broward County. He often appeared in our court arguing constitutional-law issues. I found his presentations to be knowledgeable and persuasive.

Vice President Gore was represented by three lawyers, two of whom lived in Tallahassee, and I knew them well. Dexter Douglass was a longtime successful trial lawyer. He was close friends with Governor Lawton Chiles and the governor's wife, Rhea. Dexter served as Governor Chiles's legal counsel for most of the governor's second term. Dexter helped me during the appointment process when I was appointed to the court in 1994. During my time on the court, he had made several arguments. His style was to be quite direct and dramatic, always stating his positions with great certainty as to their correctness. In the oral argument, however, Dexter's role was only to introduce counsel who would make the substantive argument for the Gore side. I had no doubt that Dexter had played a greater role in the preparation of the briefs and the preparation for the argument. John Newton was the president of the local bar association in Tallahassee for the year after I was appointed to the court. John lived in the neighborhood in which Linda and I rented a house, and we became friends. The third Gore lawyer was David Boies, whom I did not know personally, but I did know that he had wide experience in important cases of national and international importance and had an extraordinary reputation for his preparation and presentation skills.

Attorney General Bob Butterworth had filed papers. I, of course, knew him both professionally and socially. The attorney general did not himself argue cases before our court, and to my knowledge did not himself write briefs filed in the court. As was his usual practice, he had an assistant attorney general present the argument on behalf of the attorney general. The assistant attorney general who appeared on the brief in the case was George Wass, a longtime veteran of the attorney general's office who regularly appeared before the court and was always well prepared.

Governor Bush was represented by several lawyers. Barry Richard was someone I had known for many years. I first knew him when he was in the state legislature from Miami-Dade in the early 1980s. I had tried to help him when he had been a candidate for attorney general. After moving to Tallahassee, I visited with him at various social functions. He regularly made arguments before the court and was well liked and respected by all the justices. Benjamin Ginsberg, George Terwilliger, and Michael Carvin were from national law firms. I did not know them, but, like Boies, they had excellent reputations in cases of national and international significance.

Secretary Katherine Harris was represented by her general counsel, Deborah Kearney, and by Joe Klock from Miami. I knew that both of these lawyers had excellent reputations, but I did not know either of them personally.

I thought that the parties had chosen well and that the legal talent was indeed impressive. I read all the papers carefully for the rest of Saturday and most of Sunday. Though the lawyers presented different legal arguments, I came away from this review with the same basic understanding and thoughts with which I had begun the weekend's study.

The briefs spent considerable time and energy attacking and defending the conduct and decisions of Secretary Harris and the State Department of Elections. I did not find either side very helpful in these arguments, and I did not think this decision would turn on the motives and actions of Secretary Harris. However, following a week of judicial conferences, I was aware that several of the justices did feel strongly that Secretary Harris's conduct and actions were politically motivated in favor of Bush to the detriment of the counting of votes. Their comments in our conferences left no doubt in my mind about this. I had those same feelings, although I did not believe my feelings were as strong in this regard as those of some other members of the court.

I thought the briefs were helpful in their arguments about the construction of the statutes. Gore's argument was that in our court's earlier decisions in election controversies, the court had stressed the importance of the will of the voters prevailing over technical adherence to the letter of the election law. In deciding a case arising out of a close congressional election, the court stated: "the electorate effecting its will through its balloting, not through the hyper compliance with statutes, is the object of holding an election."[3] Gore argued that this core principle meant that there did not have to be and should not be a technical adherence to the Subsection .111 deadline to the detriment of counting uncounted ballots.

In response, Bush pointed to the 1998 opinion I had written in the case involving a sheriff's election in which the opinion said that the court's election decisions should not be read as condoning anything less by election officials than adhering to the statutorily mandated election procedures.[4] This apparent conflict meant to me nothing more than that our court in deciding election cases in the past had been influenced by the factual setting of a particular case, but had consistently held that the prime goal of the court's decisions was to find a way for the will of the voters to prevail.

Gore argued that historically our court had made the rights of voters paramount in resolving election disputes. Bush responded that the statutes had to be given their literal meaning and that adherence to the seven-day deadline was mandatory. Bush and Harris argued that adherence to the express statutory deadline was the only way that resolution of the disputes could be accomplished within the time period prior to the meeting of the presidential electors in December. Bush and Harris highlighted the importance of getting the protest phase concluded,

---

3   *Chappell v. Martinez* 536 So.2d 1007 (Fla. 1988).

4   *Beckstrom v. Volusia County Canvassing Board* 707 So.2d 720 (Fla. 1998).

of moving on to the contest phase under the election statutes, and of finality in resolving election controversies in presidential elections.

Toward the end of the Bush brief, the following was set out as an argument. It would later be more broadly made by Bush to the U.S. Supreme Court: "federal law also places additional constraints on courts that require them strictly to adhere to the legislature's prescribed manner for conducting an election to choose the state's presidential electors." The Bush argument was that there could be no change in the election law after the date of the election, and that not adhering to the seven-day deadline was a change in the law. This argument did not acknowledge the obvious conflicts in the statutes.

Gore's reply again centered upon the need to reconcile the statutory conflicts in a way that would allow counting of votes so that the will of the voters would prevail. Gore also sought for our court to set standards to be used by the counters in manually counting the votes. In the end, the absence of such standards in the statutes turned out to be a crucial factor in the case. In reading Gore's brief, I was surprised that this was first raised by his legal team in the reply brief. Reply briefs are to be limited to what has been argued in the other party's answer briefs and by the issues that were before the court whose order is the subject to the appeal. That was not the situation here. The issue of standards was first raised in the Broward County Canvassing Board's intervener brief.

Moreover, I thought that the setting of standards was actually a legislative prerogative and would require the input of election experts to advise as to the pros and cons of what those standards should be. I did not think our court had a sufficient record to set such standards even if it was within our power to do so. For these reasons, I did not at that time give much thought to the setting of standards for the manual counting of ballots.

By Sunday afternoon around 4:30 p.m., I had completed reading the vast amount of written material that had been provided to me and had reached a level of diminishing returns in absorbing it. My mind was becoming numb, so I headed for home with the idea that I would complete my preparation when I arrived at the court early Monday morning.

11

Oral Argument

At exactly 2:05 p.m. from behind the curtain to the justices' entry to the courtroom I heard Marshal Barnes's familiar voice boom out the court's call to order: "Hear ye, hear ye, hear ye—all rise—God bless the United States, the Great State of Florida, and this honorable court—Ladies and Gentlemen, the Florida Supreme Court!"

We entered the courtroom. As chief justice, I was first through the curtain, followed, in order of seniority, by Justices Shaw, Harding, Anstead, Pariente, Lewis, and Quince. The courtroom had no spare seats and was silent, reflecting the solemnity and tension of the occasion.

As I stood at my seat on the bench waiting for the marshal to say, "Please be seated," I looked down on the sheet prepared for me by Marshal Barnes that listed the names of counsel who had advised the marshal that they would present argument. I faced the courtroom. At the counsel table on my right was Mr. Paul Hancock, appearing on behalf of Attorney General Robert Butterworth; Mr. Bruce Rogow, counsel for the Palm Beach Canvassing Board; Mr. David Boies for the vice president; and at the end of that table was Mr. Dexter Douglass for the vice president. Sitting in the first row of the gallery behind that counsel table was the familiar face of former U.S. secretary of state Warren Christopher, who I had read in the news reports was working with the Gore team.

Immediately in front of me was the rostrum from which counsel would address their arguments to the court.

At the counsel table to my left were Mr. Michael Carvin and Mr. Barry Richard, appearing for Governor Bush. To the left in the row behind the counsel table, but in front of the bar that separated counsel from the gallery, was Mr. Joseph Klock, appearing for Secretary Harris. Behind them at the end of the front row of the gallery was former U.S. secretary of state James Baker, who I knew from news reports was working with the Bush team.

In the second row of the gallery immediately behind Secretary of State Baker were the justices' spouses. Marshal Barnes had made certain that our spouses had seats. Also seated on that row were some of our former justices and their spouses. On my right in the first several rows were news reporters who had been picked for the pool of seats we had by agreement reserved for a limited number of media representatives. On the sides of the courtroom, a limited number of still photographers had been set up. There was no video recording visible in the courtroom. Rather, as planned, the videotaping was done through the portals at the back of the courtroom near the ceiling.

We knew that there would be great demand to be in the courtroom for the argument, and that the line would form early. In fact, by 8:00 a.m., looking out the windows of my office, I could see that a substantial line had formed. We had reserved seats for the governor and other cabinet officers. Neither Governor Jeb Bush nor Secretary Harris was present. There were many members of the legislature present. Naturally, legislators were interested in watching this historic oral argument. I thought to myself that part of the legislators' interest in being present at the oral argument without question was that they wanted to signal to our court that they were in Tallahassee and paying close attention to what we were doing.

(The following excerpts are from the real-time transcript of the oral argument):

I spoke:

The court is certainly aware of the historic nature of this session and this is a matter of utmost and vital importance to our nation and to our state and our world. . . . We appreciate the diligence that counsel has taken in getting all of these issues framed and to us. Since we have a limited amount of time here, we would ask that we get to the heart of the matter.

I recognized Mr. Hancock to begin his argument.

Mr. Hancock began with a general statement about the importance of voters. I quickly broke in and attempted to focus him on my number-one concern, which was the ultimate deadline. I wanted the lawyers to tell us their positions as to by what date Florida's electoral votes would be prejudiced if the entire controversy was not resolved. I did not want the controversies in the Florida courts to continue so long that Florida's electoral votes would not be included when the presidential electors gathered to cast their votes for president.

Mr. Hancock finally answered that the date was December 12, 2000. I repeated the question to each of the other attorneys as to the specific date. By the end of the argument, all had answered—December 12, 2000. Thus, I believed that the question about the deadline for the controversy was resolved.

The argument moved forward to the completion of Mr. Hancock's presentation, brief comments by Mr. Rogow on behalf of the Palm Beach County Canvassing Board and Mr. Andrew Meyer on behalf of the Broward County Canvassing Board, and on to Mr. Boies. As I thought would happen, each justice zeroed in on the statutory construction of Subsection .111 and .112, and how the timing of manual recounts under the protest statute could be reconciled with the seven-day deadline in heavily populated counties in south Florida. Justices Anstead, Pariente, and Quince each asked questions that implied criticism of Secretary Harris's construction of the statutes, and the role of the State Division of Elections in the recounts starting and stopping.

Justice Lewis asked a question of Mr. Boies that touched upon my concern that we were dealing with only the protest phase of the controversies when the statute also provided for the contest phase:

> We have the 166 (F.S.102.166) recount and the full statutory scheme, but we also have the 168 (F.S.102.168) section for contesting those results, and if this contesting continues up to the eve of reporting to the Electoral College, would we then write out, would we not, the provision for contesting what is a recount?

Justice Lewis later added:

What I am concerned about is the timing. . . . Let's assume that the absentees and recounts come to the eve of the reporting day and there is insufficient time, just as a matter of fact, to conduct a contest, so then are we not eliminating 168.168 from our statutory scheme?

Mr. Boies answered:

I think you would be if that happened.

Mr. Boies further elaborated on his answer and then said:

I also think this court certainly has the power to say what we are going to do is tell the county boards that you have this amount of time to complete your recount and at that point those votes are then subject to being contested by Governor Bush or Vice President Gore; and those contests then take place in a time frame that allows everything to be completed by December 12, 2000. So I think it is clearly within the power of this court to say in order to meet the date of December 12, 2000, you have to have all your votes manually counted that are going to be included in this initial certification by a particular date, and then the contest, if there is one, takes place between that date and December 18, 2000.

I did not understand Mr. Boies interchanging December 12 and 18 in his answer. However, I did not focus long on that because Justice Harding followed with what I thought were the ultimate and most difficult questions for our decision:

Do we have information in the record that can guide us? Do we know how long it is going to take to do each of these things? Are we just going to reach up for some inspiration and put it down on paper?

Mr. Boies responded:

Your honor, I think it is in between; I think there is some information in the record, but to be completely candid with the Court I believe that there is going to be a lot of judgment applied by the court as well . . .

The sum of Mr. Boies's contention was that though there was not guidance for fixing of a new date, the seven-day deadline in the statutory subsections was not an end date for counting ballots because the statute did not prohibit the returns received by the end of the seven days being supplemented. He said he would leave it to the judgment of the court as to when the deadline date for supplemental returns would be.

I was impressed by Mr. Boies's easy and pleasant manner. I thought that the point about the returns being supplemented after the seven days had some merit. However, I was troubled by his not having a response to Justice Harding's questions. In the end, if the court set a deadline for supplements to the returns, the court was left to a large degree with what Justice Harding termed "reaching up for inspiration."

Before he sat down, Mr. Boies was questioned by Justices Pariente and Quince about standards for manual recounts of the punch-card ballots involving the chads. This was the argument that had been raised in the Gore reply brief, and in the Broward County Canvassing Board's intervener brief. As I stated previously, I did not think the court should consider the issue of standards in deciding the case before us. I recognized, however, that Justices Pariente and Quince did, and that whether the court could and would set such standards was going to be intensely discussed during our postargument conference.

As his time ended, Mr. Boies addressed the Bush argument that undertaking manual recounts only in the three populated south Florida counties that were heavily Democratic was unfairly partisan. Mr. Boies responded that Gore was willing for the court to set a period in which recounts in additional counties could be requested. I did not take either side's argument on this point very seriously. Neither side was requesting a statewide recount.

When Mr. Boies sat down, we took a ten-minute recess. Usually in an hour's oral argument you get to a point in which you wonder, "When is this going to end?" That did not happen in this hour. To the contrary, I was surprised that we were at the end of an hour.

During the recess, there was little chatter in the conference room. Everyone was concentrating on what they had heard and looking at their notes. Promptly when the ten minutes were up we filed back into the courtroom, again in order of seniority.

The argument resumed with Secretary Harris's counsel, Mr. Joseph Klock, who made the following point early in his presentation: "The difference we have here is really not a legal problem; it is a political problem."

I sloughed off this comment as a political jab at the opposition. After the fact, though, I slowly realized that this statement probably succinctly encapsulated the reality of the situation.

The reality was that the battle by both sides at this stage was directed at the certification of the winner. This was not because of the legal significance of that certification. Rather, each side believed that certification of Bush as the winner would likely have a substantial, perhaps conclusive effect, on the media's opinion, thereby on public opinion and consequently on the views of Democratic Party leaders not directly on the Gore team. This could be decisive in determining whether those leaders believed Gore's legal battle should continue. In the end, a case concerning an election, especially the election for president of the United States, is about politics. Naturally, the case is driven by political considerations. In many ways from start to finish, this case was, as Mr. Klock said, a political problem more than a legal problem.

I asked Mr. Klock how Secretary Harris was protecting Florida's long-established policy that the interest of voters in an election was paramount:

> The concern I have is that we have a long-standing policy out of the courts of this state, that state the real parties in interest here are the voters. Now what I want to know—and this is 112 (F.S.102.112) has a provision which says that some voters' votes may be ignored—what is the boundaries upon which the Secretary could exercise discretion and have those voters ignored—in this particular presidential election, doesn't it revolve around the Electoral College and the prejudice of not allowing Florida votes counted?

I later added:

> What I am concerned with now is the rights of the voters who may not have their votes counted if we don't honor the recounted

votes and the rights of all the voters who might have their rights denied if the certification doesn't get in within the time limit and on the basis that it will be accepted under Title 5 of the U.S. Code.

Mr. Klock responded that the only bar to the votes being certified was the "stay" our court had entered preventing Secretary Harris from certifying the winner. Mr. Klock further argued that once the certification was made, but not until then, the contests authorized by Section 102.168 of the Florida Statutes could be undertaken to test the validity of the recounts. The logic of this was that the court should remove the stay, allow the certification, and then the contests could begin. Such a conclusion obviously served Bush's interest since he would be certified as the winner.

As Mr. Klock continued, he was cross-examined closely by Justices Anstead, Pariente, and Quince with what I thought were hostile questions concerning Secretary Harris's refusal to accept supplemental returns. Mr. Klock's core response was that in order to find that Secretary Harris had abused her discretion, the court had to do "a great deal of legislating." I knew that his answers were not persuading his interrogators. I doubted that any answer on behalf of Secretary Harris would. My impression was that these questions were the verbal expressions of their feeling, with which I agreed, that Secretary Harris's actions were influenced by her political role during the campaign.

Next up was Mr. Michael Carvin on behalf of Bush. Early in his response to questions from the justices, Mr. Carvin stated that recounting only three counties selected by one political party was unfairly partisan. This statement was quickly challenged by Justice Pariente's fair question as to whether he was requesting a recount in the other sixty-four counties, and why his client had not sought a recount in other counties.

Mr. Carvin replied:

They believe the process is inherently flawed and unconstitutional . . .

Justice Pariente followed:

> So even if we said everyone has a chance for a window to request a recount in whatever other counties are in question, are you saying that is the position of Governor Bush?

Mr. Carvin didn't hesitate:

> Yes, I am. . . . I think we should follow the process set out in the statute.

Justice Pariente:

> What part of the process is flawed?

Mr. Carvin:

> We think the process is entirely subjective, subject to mischief.

Justice Shaw then followed with a precise question:

> Do I understand your previous answer to be that you would not be interested in opening up this window of opportunity under any circumstances (recount of all the votes) since you believe the system is flawed?

Mr. Carvin:

> My answer is that anything that departs from the rules that were set before November 7, 2000, before the election, by the Florida legislature would be a gross abuse of discretion and impermissible, and that is why we have deadlines and that is why we have uniform rules, because we want election contests to be decided, not in this fevered partisan environment where everyone knows the way they proceed in counting ballots or whether they use a two corner rule versus dimple ballot it may well affect the outcome of the election because that introduces subjectivity and partisanship into it. That is the reason why it is important that we follow the rules set forth by statute that were written by the legislature long ago.

Justice Quince pressed Mr. Carvin as to whether he meant that under no circumstances would a manual recount be proper. He responded:

My point is that you don't have the voter in front of you. You have the ballot in front of you. And what needs to be done is look at the ballot, pursuant to some subjective criteria and determine whether or not the punch is sufficiently strong showing that the voter intended to do that, to figure out whether or not they intended it. But, as we know, and the colloquy before indicates, that is a standardless inquiry which there are no Florida rules on and that is why they are asking you for some guidance. My point is[,] how can this court, after the election has been held[,] start deciding on resetting the statutory deadlines, reanalyzing the statutory terms for resolving empirical questions of the sort that you are discussing, and redoing everything that reflects a considered judgment that is already in the election code?

To which Justice Quince rejoined:

But that sounds like you are coming back to all these ballots would just not be counted, all of those voters would be disenfranchised.

In answer to a question by Justice Quince, Mr. Carvin summed up his argument:

I would urge that the court not, after the election has been held, change the rules by which the election should be conducted.

I did not realize it at the time, but with the benefit of hindsight, I believe that within those exchanges was the foundation of Bush's United States constitutional argument, and ultimately the basis of the decision by the U.S. Supreme Court on December 12, 2000.

The essence of this argument was that the statute did not provide standards for the performing of manual recounts of ballots, and that what our court did in construing the election statutes to allow for recounts changed the law after the election in violation of the U.S. Constitution and federal statutory law. This "change the law after the election occurred" contention was buried in both the Bush brief and oral argument amid the focus upon the conduct of Secretary Harris, and the conflicts in the election statutes. It was not apparent to me at the time that Bush's argument was intended to be rooted in federal law.

In fact, it was not until I had advised Mr. Carvin that the Bush side's time for argument was close to ending, and that he should allow his Florida cocounsel, Mr. Barry Richard, to use the closing minutes (which had been requested by Mr. Carvin and Mr. Richard before the argument began), that the impact of federal law was even mentioned by Mr. Carvin. Mr. Richard, when he closed for the Bush side, did make the explicit point:

> I think the recounts must stop, if the seven-day cutoff occurs[,] unless the Secretary of State, in the exercise of the discretion the legislature has given her, determines there is a rational reason for them to continue. It is the job of the Secretary of State reposed in her by the legislature and the U.S. Constitution and the Florida Constitution, in unusually explicit language, have delegated that decision not to the State of Florida, not to the Courts of the State of Florida, but to the legislature of the State of Florida and the legislature of the State of Florida has reposed that authority in the Secretary of State.

This argument did become the focal point of the review of our court's decision in this case in the U.S. Supreme Court.

Following Mr. Richard, Mr. Boies rebutted the Bush arguments. He did not pick up on Mr. Carvin's or Mr. Richard's last points. Rather, Mr. Boies returned to the issue of the basis for the court's power to set a new deadline for the returns to be reported to the State:

> . . . what this court has to do is to reconcile the entire statutory scheme, and the statutory scheme long before there was this election provided for manual recounts. And this court, I suggest[,] cannot presume that the legislature meant to provide for these manual recounts and yet to make that an illusory right by having a circumstance where they could not be practically taken care of in what was the most important election that this state has perhaps ever seen. I think the standard that the Chief Justice referred to,

which is when will the date be such that passing that date endangers the ability of certifying and finalizing any contest that may result, that the votes of Florida are not in peril. And I believe that that is not an issue in this particular situation because the counties have said that if you will give—if you will tell us what the standard is and leave us free from interference, we can get this done in a matter of days; now Broward County stopped because they were told to stop, then started again after this court said they could start, you know what happened? A Republican official or a Republican attorney subpoenaed the canvassing Board to a circuit court and the counting had to stop.

Mr. Boies continued with his wrap-up, and then sat down.

Oral arguments were now completed. Marshal Barnes barked out, "All rise," and the justices stood and receded from the courtroom through the curtains through which we had entered.

We went directly into our downstairs conference room and hung our robes in their assigned closets. Everyone took a short break. It was close to 5:00 p.m. when the members of the court took their designated seats at the conference table. We usually began our deliberations on a case immediately following the oral argument. Obviously there was nothing usual in this instance. I wanted to put over deliberations until the next morning. We were all tired from our long preparation and the tension of the event. The next morning we would be fresh. Others, though, wanted to begin right away. I acceded to the others, and we started with our discussion. As was our custom, we went from justice to justice in order of seniority discussing various points for about two hours. We were not close to finishing our discussion of issues at the end of two hours. At that point, I insisted upon a twenty-minute break to return to our offices.

When we returned to the conference room after the office break, I again urged that we recess for the evening. At this time, a majority agreed to start again the next morning. We recessed.

The exact time when we could get started the next day was complicated by obligations that Major Harding and I had to swear in members of the House and Senate who were meeting in the initial organization sessions of the term. I was to swear in the incoming Speaker and members of the House. Justice Harding was to swear in the president of the Senate and new senators. These times had been agreed to months before. I explained this complication to the other justices and told them that our conference would likely be able to begin at 11:00 a.m., but to please wait in their chambers. I advised that I would call them when Justice Harding and I returned from the legislature.

Before I departed the court, I met with Marshal Barnes. He reported that all had gone smoothly with security. Craig Waters came in and gave me a report on the media, noting that all appeared satisfied with the arrangements. We discussed the next day. Marshal Barnes said he would arrange to take Justice Harding and me across to the Capitol Building in a law-enforcement vehicle. Even though the legislature was meeting right across the street, the crowds in front of the court would be a problem for our walking across to the Capitol.

Finally I was alone and had the time and the silence in which to think about what I had heard in the argument. I thought the arguments revealed that the justices were struggling with the issues embedded in the statutory deadlines. I was surprised that more of the argument did not discuss Circuit Judge Lewis's order. After all, it was that order from which the appeal had been taken. I did think that the argument properly focused upon protecting the rights of voters, both those whose votes had not been counted and those who votes had been counted.

I had gone into oral argument leaning toward the view that Secretary Harris had unreasonably interfered with the counting of the votes in Palm Beach and Broward Counties. I thought that fairness and the rights of the voters pointed toward extending the deadlines in those counties. I did not fully grasp what had happened in Miami-Dade County to cause the canvassing board to start and then to stop the manual counting. Unfortunately, the arguments did not strengthen my understanding.

I was not impressed with Bush's argument, made at the end of the arguments by Mr. Carvin and Mr. Richard, that the court did not have the power to act because to do so would be changing the election law after the election. The conflicts in the statutes required the court to act. The controversy had to be resolved by statutory construction when that could be done, and then by coming to a reasonable new deadline based upon balancing the need for more time to count the punch-card ballots to complete the statutory protests and the time required after the completion of the protests for the statutory contests to be processed and finally resolved. I was dedicated to protecting the rights of all the voters who cast ballots in every practical way under the circumstances and time requirements.

I came out of the argument agreeing with Mr. Klock that the contest phase had to start at an early time. My impression from the comments by the other justices, both from their questions during the oral arguments and our two hours of post–oral argument discussions, was that all were for continuing the counting. How long we should allow the counting to continue would be the issue that could divide us.

I also knew from the questions and our discussion that some of the justices wanted to set a standard to be used for recounting the ballots. I continued to believe that the court should not and could not do that. I was even firmer in my belief that setting such standards was for the legislature to do, and that we had no record upon which to set such standards even if setting such standards could be found to be within the reasonable and proper judicial powers of the court. To set such standards would require expertise as to the punch-card ballots and chad problems. Such expertise had not been developed in the record in the case. Furthermore, the standards for counting were not part of the case before the circuit court. What our court would be doing in setting standards would be issuing an advisory opinion, which our jurisdiction did not authorize and was not within our expertise. Finally, setting standards now, after the election, would be creating the election rules after the election had taken place. I knew, however, that the lack of standards for manual counting of ballots was a crucial problem, and would be a recurring matter of contention.

I went home. The next day was going to be just as eventful as this day had been. Even though we could not start our deliberations until late morning, we had to issue a decision with an opinion that day.

12

Decision in the Protest Case

After the argument, my thoughts about the case solidified overnight. We had to deal practically with the situations confronting us. Confusion and uncertainty surrounded the counting and certification of ballots in three major Florida counties. The election statutes were in conflict. Secretary Harris had not reasonably exercised the discretion that a proper construction of the conflicting election statutes provided to her. The punch-card ballots had inherent problems. The time for ending the protest phase of the election disputes was rapidly approaching so that any contests could begin and be processed within the federal law and constitutional time constraints.

I worked to shape my conclusion within my fundamental philosophy that the court should adhere as closely as it reasonably could to what the legislature had written in the statutes. My first choice always was to give strict literal construction to statutes. During my years on the court, I had grown increasingly wary of the court varying from the language of a statute because it left too much room for a court majority, as thin as one vote, to substitute its judgment for that of the legislature.

In looking at the present case, however, I did not see a way to give literal construction to what the legislature had written in the election laws and come to a resolution that met the test of good common sense and logic. The statutes simply had too many conflicts. There was no way to give literal meaning to two statutes—one of which said, "shall ignore," and the other of which said, "may ignore." There was no way to give literal construction to statutes that provided a right to order recounts right up to the deadline for reporting vote counts, but left no time for doing the recount before the returns were directed to be ignored.

The mess with the statutes was superimposed on a form of the ballot that was itself a mess. As had become abundantly clear, the punch-card ballot was at the root of the controversy in each of the three counties in dispute. During the oral argument, Justice Quince had asked questions that pointed out that there were just too many punch-card ballots with chad problems for the problems to be explained on the basis that the voters did not follow instructions. In addition, these punch-card ballots had given rise to litigation in other states involving similar chad problems in elections before the 2000 presidential election, which was a clear indication that the ballots, not the voters, were the problem.

I did not know if manual counting of the punch-card ballots would straighten out the mess, but I thought that Secretary Harris should have given the county canvassing boards more time to do manual counting of the ballots. The length of the extended period of time had to be bounded by a date that would safeguard against the loss of Florida's right to cast its electoral votes when the votes of electors from all the other states were cast on December 18, 2000. It seemed to me quite sensible that Secretary Harris's discretion was in reality limited by the time that the manual counting could continue in this protest phase of the postelection and still leave sufficient time for the contest phase of the election statutes to be pursued to final resolution without prejudicing Florida's electoral votes.

My decision in the case before us required me to determine the proper extension period for counting. I jotted down my time calculations on a legal pad. Applying the strict seven-day statutory time period, plus the additional three days that the State had agreed to for the receipt of overseas ballots, brought me to November 18, 2000, which was the date when Secretary Harris had stated that she was going to certify the winner. This was her decision, which we had stayed in the order we issued when the case first arrived at our court. The time between November 18, 2000, and the December 12, 2000, deadline for finally resolving all controversies came to twenty-four days. This would have been the amount of time, according to the positions of Secretary Harris and Governor Bush, in which contests under Section 102.168 could be processed and decided by the circuit court and final appeals completed in the appellate courts.

With our stay order we had already extended the initial time period at least through the present date, which was November 21, 2000. I concluded that the court had to set a new deadline because the only other alternatives were to merely lift the stay and allow immediate certification, as Mr. Klock had urged in his argument, or direct Secretary Harris to determine an extended time. I rejected simply lifting the stay because I had concluded that Secretary Harris had abused her discretion in not extending the time, and it would have been unfair to Vice President Gore, and to the canvassing boards that were trying to do recounts, to simply hold that the manual counting would immediately have to stop despite the abuse of discretion. Importantly, I thought that there was some leeway in the time still remaining until December 12, 2000, during which the votes of the punch-card ballots could be manually counted and not jeopardize the votes of other voters who were not caught up in the counting problem. I thought that we did have the time to allow the county canvassing boards in Palm Beach, Broward, and Miami-Dade to manually count votes that the canvassing boards determined had not been counted because of the defect inherent in the punch-card ballots without jeopardizing Florida's votes in the presidential Electoral College.

I did not think that directing Secretary Harris to set a new time was practical because that would just delay making a date certain as to when the manual counting had to be completed and the contest could begin. Additionally, I thought that whatever the extended date set by Secretary Harris, it would very likely be considered by Gore's team to be political, and the secretary's decision would again become the subject of an appeal.

I fully understood that there were problems with the court setting a new date. The hard question that Justice Harding had so aptly asked was on what basis the court could set a new date. The question had not been answered, and the court was left to figure out the answer. For me, the conclusion was inescapable: the court needed to balance the time remaining until December 12, 2000, and settle upon a reasonable extended time for voters to have their votes counted. I did not like for the court to exercise such unbridled power in determining and applying a statutory scheme. I concluded, however, that this was the only practical commonsense resolution of the problem presented by the facts of the case before us.

I decided the criterion necessary to make this decision was to provide time to wrap up manual counting, and still leave time to file, process, and finalize contests. So, I wrote down on paper an ending date of the end of the workday on November 24, 2000. That would be the Friday after Thanksgiving. This would leave eighteen days for the contests. I thought that, under the circumstances, this was sufficient time for processing any contests and that the contests could reasonably be finalized by the December 12, 2000, deadline.

By the time I finished thinking this through and doing my time calculations, it was 9:40 a.m. At that time, Justice Harding and I, dressed in our robes, met in the garage of the Supreme Court Building, got into a Florida Department of Law Enforcement vehicle, and were driven across the street into the basement garage of the Capitol Building. Justice Harding was then escorted to the Senate chambers to swear in the new Senate president and members. I was escorted to the House to swear in the new Speaker and members of the House of Representatives.

It was close to noon before Justice Harding and I could return to the court. I sent word to the other justices that we would meet in the conference room at 1:00 p.m. When the conference began, we wasted no time in getting into the discussions of the issues. Little time passed before it became clear that we were all in agreement on the basic issues. We agreed that the statutes were in conflict and had to be construed, that Secretary Harris was wrong in restricting the reasons that the time deadlines could be extended, and that her decision to reject the manual recounts and certify the election on November 18, 2000, was an abuse of discretion. Thus, we concluded that Circuit Judge Lewis's decision was to be reversed. We then agreed that this meant that we would have to settle upon an extended deadline.

There were issues upon which there was not agreement. One issue was the setting of standards for manually counting the ballots. We had a long discussion about this. For the reasons I have previously set out,

I did not think that the court could set standards in the present case. Others did not agree. There was extensive discussion about whether the "intent of the voter" was a standard, and several justices were strongly of the view that the court should, in the opinion deciding the case, state that the "intent of the voter" was the Florida standard. I did not agree that that was a standard which would facilitate manual counting of the ballots. Deciding the "intent of the voter" would too often be nothing more than the subjective opinion of the person doing the manual counting. In the end, the decision was made that we should not set standards. I think that all the justices came to recognize that the setting of standards was not part of the case before Circuit Judge Lewis and had not been argued by the parties to the case until the reply briefs, and that there was a lack of a consensus among the justices as to what the standards, if set, would be.

We then had a long discussion of the extended deadline date. Most of the justices wanted to extend the time well beyond the November 24, 2000, date that I had favored. We finally settled on 5:00 p.m. on Sunday, November 26, 2000, if Secretary Harris's office was open to receive the returns at that time. We did not know whether she would, in fact, open the office on that Sunday to accept the returns, so we set an alternative deadline of 9:00 a.m. on Monday morning. The justices differed substantially as to the new deadline, but all the justices believed that unanimity was extremely important in this case.

The other difficult task of the afternoon was coming to an agreement on the opinion that would be issued with the decision. The drafting of the opinion was unique in my experience, with the justices all sitting around the conference table preparing it. For more than six hours, we collectively worked through the opinion word by word.

By 6:30 p.m., the opinion was ready for final edits. The justices then agreed upon a statement summarizing the decision and the opinion that would be read by Craig Waters. We agreed that Marshal Barnes should give the media thirty minutes' advance warning that an opinion was about to issue that evening.

Although we were going to release the opinion online, the procedure for release was that we would also provide printed copies to the media waiting outside the building for the release. Unfortunately, at the time the opinion was about to be released online, the clerk's office copier went down. It took another thirty minutes to find another copier in the building and get the opinion copied. Finally, the decision and opinion were released around 8:30 p.m.

As the opinion was being copied and released, I sat alone in my office. I was generally pleased with the decision and the opinion. There was certainly language in the opinion that, if I had written the opinion alone, I would not have included, and language omitted that I would have included. But this was a true *per curiam* opinion[1]—an opinion by the court. In sum, I thought our opinion was well stated. We implemented a long-accepted principle in Florida election law that the rights of voters were to take precedence and be safeguarded, and we determined a date that was fair to those voters whose votes had not been counted, while protecting the statutory right to further contest the election within a time period that would preserve Florida's electoral votes. I was quite satisfied.

I assumed, without knowing, that a clear majority of the members of the court favored the election of Vice President Gore. But I did not think that favoritism toward Gore drove the decision or the opinion.

About 9:00 p.m., I went home. By the time I got home, both Gore and Bush representatives were filling the radio and television with statements. The Gore team was praising the opinion. The Bush team was blasting it. Frankly, I was somewhat taken aback by the vehemence with which the Bush supporters were attacking our court and the opinion. But that was the way it was.

---

1   *Palm Beach County Canvassing Board v. Harris* 772 So.2d 1220 (Fla. 2000).

13

An Eventful Thanksgiving

It was the day before Thanksgiving. Linda and I had long planned to spend the holidays with our family at the home of our daughter Shelley and her husband, Bill, which was an apartment located on Brickell Key in Miami. Shelley and Bill were both training to be doctors at Miami's Jackson Hospital. Our son Talley and his wife, Laura, and our daughter Ashley were going to join us there.

When oral argument had been scheduled for Monday, I realized that I might have to stay through Wednesday in Tallahassee. We decided that Linda would go ahead of me on Wednesday morning, and I arranged to fly to Miami on Wednesday evening.

Driving to the court that morning, I listened to the radio and heard further criticism from Bush's team of our decision. I heard and then read statements from former U.S. secretary of state James Baker, Representative Tom DeLay, and Representative Dick Armey. I thought the statement by Representative Joe Scarborough from Pensacola was among the most strident:[1]

> Tonight the Florida Supreme Court declared war on the rule of law in Florida. Seven radical Democratic lawyers have chosen to ignore the clear intent of Florida's legislative and executive branches. If it is a political war they want, it is a political war they should get.

I hoped Joe Scarborough had not read the statutes or the court's opinion when he made that statement. I did not know him, but the senior

---

1   *St. Petersburg Times*, November 22, 2000, 7-A.

partner in the law firm he had been associated with in Pensacola before he went to Congress was an excellent lawyer and longtime friend of mine. Since he had worked for that law firm, I was disappointed in Joe Scarborough's quoted statement. At the same time, I realized that everything the politicians were saying, certainly including Joe Scarborough, was political rhetoric, not legal analysis.

The justices met in the chief's office on Wednesday morning at 10:00 a.m. Before we scattered for the holidays, we needed to make a plan in the event that something was filed that required the court's immediate attention. At this gathering there was a general feeling of relaxation. We had released our opinion, and the pressure that had been increasingly on us since the day after the election was relieved, at least for the moment. I cautioned the group to keep in mind that this was only half-time. I fully expected a contest by the side with the fewest votes when the extended deadline for certification of the winner passed. I did not suspect, nor do I think any of justices suspected at the time of that conference, how soon the pressure would again be upon us.

After our morning meeting, I decided I could continue with my plans to fly to Miami on Wednesday evening to be there for Thanksgiving. Marshal Barnes thought that I should have security protection when I arrived at the Miami airport. Upon arriving in Miami, I was met by representatives of the Florida Department of Law Enforcement as well as airport security officers. The officers surrounded me and escorted me through the airport. I think the people who saw me thought I must be a fugitive or in a witness-protection program. No one seemed to recognize me from my television appearance the day before.

After I arrived at Shelley and Bill's apartment, I saw television reports that there had been dramatic developments at the Miami-Dade courthouse while I was flying to Miami. Television reports stated that a meeting of the Miami-Dade County Canvassing Board had ended with a majority of the canvassing board voting not to continue the manual counting of the ballots. The reason stated for the majority's vote was that the majority concluded that it was impossible to complete a manual counting of the ballots by the 5:00 p.m. Sunday deadline set in our November 21 decision. The number of ballots which had been cast in Miami-Dade was reportedly in excess of 600,000. The report went on to say that the Gore team had filed a petition in the Third District Court of Appeals, which is located in Dade County, seeking an order requiring the canvassing board to resume the manual counting of ballots. The Third District Court reportedly denied the petition without prejudice to Gore seeking relief from our court. I turned off the television realizing, contrary to my belief on the evening of November 21, 2000, after we issued our opinion, that the protest phase of the controversy was going to continue.

By the time I awoke early on Thanksgiving morning, television reports noted that Gore had filed an emergency motion in our court seeking to require the canvassing board to continue manually counting the ballots. The reports also were that Bush was going to file a petition in the U.S. Supreme Court seeking to overturn the decision that we had issued on November 21, 2000.

Newspapers were filled with more political comments and columnists' analysis of our opinion. There were also reports that Speaker of the Florida House of Representatives Tom Feeney planned to call a special legislative session to select a slate of presidential electors. The Bush team was making a lot of noise about our court having gone too far and changing the election law after the election. Opposing those views were newspaper editorials and opinion columns condemning our decision for not providing enough time and clear standards for the manual counting of ballots. There were many writers who said that we should have ordered a statewide recount.

I mulled over these reports and comments for about an hour. I again pondered, as I had when I heard the comments by Joe Scarborough, whether the comments were from politicians, editorial writers, and columnists who had actually read the statutes, understood that the statutory scheme had both protest and contest phases, and read our opinion. I thought that, if the commentators had done those things and employed even moderate objectivity, the commentary would have been different.

I thought much of the critical political and news media commentary was also based upon a different concept of the role of our court than mine. I regarded the court's jurisdiction to be limited. The Florida Constitution did not give the court the power to reach out for cases and issues to decide. The Florida Supreme Court is, at its most fundamental, an appellate court that reviews decisions made by a lower court on issues presented to the lower court by the lawyers and the parties. The court's appellate review, as it was in this case, is bounded by the record developed in the lower court, and the facts as resolved in the lower court. The court does not call witnesses, admit evidence, or make decisions regarding the credibility of witnesses.

Because I thought these limitations on the court's power had to be respected, I continued to believe we had been correct in not setting standards for counting and in not ordering a statewide recount. My reasons for not taking such actions continued to be that the lower court had not dealt with the standards issue, and there was no factual or expert opinion on which to set standards. I continued with the view that the setting of such standards was the responsibility of the legislature. In respect to a statewide recount, no party had sought such a recount.

Shortly after 9:00 a.m., Tom Hall and Craig Waters called to tell me that the Gore petition had been filed. I told Tom Hall to contact all the justices to either fax the petition to them or read it to them. He had already circulated the petitions to the justices' offices. Many of the staff lawyers were already at the court. I told Tom to advise the justices that we would have a telephone conference call at 10:00 a.m. to discuss the petition, and how to proceed.

The members of the court were scattered. Justice Pariente was on Cape Cod in Massachusetts. Major Harding was at Calloway Gardens in Georgia. I did not remember where the other justices were. But all were reached for the conference call. I spoke from the privacy of Shelley and Bill's bedroom.

The petition stated that the canvassing board had started counting the ballots following our decision, but then had voted to stop in view of our Sunday deadline. The counting, which had been done, resulted in a net gain of 156 votes for Gore. In its order denying the petition, [2] the

---

2   *Miami-Dade County Democratic Party v. Miami-Dade Canvassing Board* 773 So.2d
     1179 (Fla. 3d DCA 2000).

district court stated: "Since the canvassing board has determined that a manual recount cannot be done within the time frame set in *Harris* [our November 21 decision] mandamus cannot lie." The district court then concluded: "The ruling is without prejudice to seek relief in the Florida Supreme Court from the court-ordered deadline and to ask the Supreme Court to fashion an equitable remedy tailored to the conditions of Miami-Dade County."

I agreed with the Third District's conclusion that a mandamus was not appropriate. A mandamus is an order by a court to an administrative government entity that it is to carry out a purely ministerial function for which the entity has responsibility and when the entity is not carrying out the function. However, a mandamus is not appropriate when the administrator has discretion to perform the function or not perform the function. Here we had expressly stated in our November 21 opinion that the decision whether to conduct a manual count was within the discretion of a county canvassing board. I did not see how we could now decide that the county canvassing board had to exercise that discretion in favor of counting. We would be simply second-guessing the canvassing board as to whether the count could be completed within the time we had set, and there was no basis to revisit our November 21 decision setting the extended deadline.

When the telephone conference began, the justices immediately launched into a discussion of the petition. After all members of the court expressed their views about the petition, the justices voted unanimously to deny the petition without prejudice. In other words, the court was not precluding issues in respect to those ballots being raised in any contests that could be brought after the protest period ended. We directed Tom Hall to issue an order that so stated. That completed our conference call, which lasted about an hour. Soon after we completed our call, I watched the television broadcast of Craig Waters reading the order from the steps of the Supreme Court Building.

I had a light lunch since our family's plan was to have our turkey early that evening. I began to watch football. The games were not very interesting so I switched to CNN to see that it was broadcasting live the developments at the Broward County courthouse. The difficulty the ballot counters were having with the different ballots because of the chads was evident without commentary. The counters plainly appeared to be having a lot of difficulty determining which ballots to count and which not to count. I watched only briefly, and then turned off the television in order to turn my attention to our family and our dinner.

Friday morning news reports discussed our denial of the Gore petition, and how this was a blow to the Gore election effort. That Friday was a beautiful late fall day in Miami, and our entire family went for a walk after breakfast. There was not much room for walking on Brickell Key so we walked along the seawall bordering Biscayne Bay. Linda was wearing a hat that I had been given on one of my visits to courts around the state, which had "Florida Chief Justice" on the front of it. As we walked along the seawall, Linda lost her balance and fell into Biscayne Bay. Fortunately she was not injured, and Bill, who was walking right behind her, immediately jumped in to assist her. We successfully got both of them out of the bay. However, my hat began floating away on the water. I thought, great, I can see the headlines now reporting that a hat with the label "Florida Chief Justice" had been found floating in Biscayne Bay. Has the chief drowned? Fortunately, we recaptured the hat.

After Linda's unexpected swim, our family went to Coconut Grove, a short distance from Brickell Key. We had lunch, did some Christmas shopping, and went to the movies. As we walked around, it seemed as if the election controversy had little public impact. Life seemed to be going on as normal during a Thanksgiving holiday weekend.

The movie ended around 4:00 p.m. As we were leaving the parking garage, I noticed that Craig Waters had called, and I called him back. Craig told me that the U.S. Supreme Court had granted the Bush petition to review our November 21 decision, and had set oral argument in the case for the following Friday, December 1, 2000.

I was shocked.

I was shocked not because the U.S. Supreme Court would decide that it should review a decision by a state court regarding the election of the president. To the contrary, I thought that the U.S. Supreme Court would review the ultimate decision in the presidential election controversy when the controversy reached finality in our court. After all, the decision at issue was who would be president of the United States, and I believed that the decision would need to have the approval of the highest court in the United States.

I was shocked because the Supreme Court decided to get into the case at the stage that it was in on that Friday. There was a strong likelihood that the petition that sought the Supreme Court to accept for review our November 21 decision would be rendered moot when the deadline expired on Sunday afternoon at 5:00 p.m. If Bush maintained his lead, there would be no case in controversy based on a petition by Bush, because he would not need any relief from the Supreme Court in respect to the certification of the winner. I was amazed that the Supreme Court had not at least waited until Sunday's certification to make a decision on Bush's petition. Simply delaying the decision for that brief time would have answered whether the petition for review it was accepting was moot.

Moreover, there was the entire contest phase to go before any resolution of controversy would be final. I added the Supreme Court to the list of those about whom I wondered whether there was an understanding of Florida's election laws. I called Craig to see if he knew any further details of the Supreme Court's action. He did not. I decided not to contact the other justices since there was nothing further for our court to do at this point.

The rest of Friday and all day Saturday were uneventful. I returned to Tallahassee Sunday morning, arriving about noon. All was quiet throughout the afternoon. The State Election Commission, with Secretary Harris presiding, convened to certify the ballots immediately when the 5:00 p.m. deadline expired. The meeting was broadcast live on television, but was then delayed when the Palm Beach Canvassing Board asked for an additional two hours to complete their counting. That request was denied, but the commission's consideration of the request for extension delayed the certification of the winner for more than two hours. At approximately 7:30 p.m., Bush was certified to be the winner.

I thought surely this made Bush's petition in the U.S. Supreme Court moot, and it would probably be dismissed and the Supreme Court's oral argument cancelled. I told Linda that now, finally, the protest phase of the election controversy was really going to end!

14

The Protest Goes to Washington; the Contest Goes Forward

All was quiet when I arrived at the court on Monday morning. I realized that the lull in the action at our court would not last long. The newspapers reported that Bush had claimed victory Sunday evening following the State Election Commission's certification of him as the winner of the election. Gore was reported to have vowed to fight on. The newspapers also reported that various election cases were headed in our direction.

However, I did not have time to be concerned about cases that were not already at the court. This was an oral argument week, so I went to work reviewing the cases that were on the oral argument schedule beginning that Tuesday.

The morning passed, and I had not received any word that Gore had filed a contest. I was beginning to think that perhaps Gore had made a decision not to contest the election. But then, right after lunch, the word came that Gore had filed a contest in the circuit court in Tallahassee. The contest case had been assigned to Judge Sandy Sauls.

I did not know Judge Sauls, other than speaking to him when I had been at a court ceremony for the swearing in of a new judge. While I remembered that Judge Sauls had stepped down as chief judge of the circuit of which Leon County was a part because of a dispute among the judges of that circuit, I had heard that Judge Sauls was a competent trial judge who ran a strict courtroom. I was impressed when following his assignment to the case that Judge Sauls had scheduled a hearing for that afternoon to work out scheduling.

That same afternoon we received the appeal from the Fourth District Court of Appeals, which passed through a decision by the circuit court in Palm Beach County in the consolidated "butterfly ballot" cases.[1] As I learned within the first days following the election, the label "butterfly" had come from the placement of candidates' names on the ballot in a way that resembled a butterfly. The allegations in the case were that, because of the placement of the names in relation to where punches were to be made, voters had been confused and votes had been cast for presidential candidate Patrick Buchanan when the voters had intended to cast their votes for Gore. However, the question framed by the Fourth District Court of Appeals was whether a recount in a presidential election limited to Palm Beach County is available under Florida and federal law.

The Palm Beach Circuit Court did not base its ruling upon whether the form of the ballot was allowed by the election statutes. Instead, the court ruled that there could not be a remedy for a defect in a presidential election under the contest statute, 102.168, Florida Statutes. Nor did the Fourth District frame the issue as to the form of the ballot. I thought the Palm Beach Circuit Court's ruling and the Fourth District had raised issues that likely would have to be considered in the contest before Judge Sauls. I needed to think through that point when Judge Sauls's case reached us. I knew that would be soon, but I doubted that the "butterfly" cases should be decided on these issues. I would raise this question at a court conference to discuss the case, which I planned to have at an early time.

The crowd outside the Supreme Court had thinned since the center of the action had moved to the Leon County courthouse. Most of the TV satellite trucks, however, remained parked across from our building. The media tents remained on the steps of the Capitol.

Late in the afternoon, Marshal Barnes came into my office and told me that he had received communications from aides of Reverend Jesse Jackson indicating that Reverend Jackson was leading a rally that

---

1   *Fladell v. Labarga* 775 So.2d 987 (4th DCA Fla. 2000).

evening at the Florida A&M University campus, which was located a short distance from the Supreme Court. Reverend Jackson planned to lead a march the following morning from the campus to the Supreme Court. Marshal Barnes said that he had been told that when the marchers arrived at the Supreme Court, several participants planned to speak. These included the Reverend Al Sharpton and Congressman Charles Rangel. This, of course, had the potential to disrupt the work of the court.

I told Marshal Barnes that no speeches were to be made from the steps of the Supreme Court, and that there could be no impediment to people who wanted to enter or leave the building. I was especially concerned that the way not be impeded for those who were going into or out of the building for the oral arguments. Marshal Barnes said he would work that out with the aides with whom he had discussions. Before I left for the evening, Marshal Barnes returned to my office and said that Reverend Jackson had agreed to respect my instructions, and that Marshal Barnes and Reverend Jackson's aides had worked out a plan in which the speeches would be on the south lawn of the building away from the entrance. On Tuesday morning, the marchers came, and the plan worked well. The speeches were made without any problems arising. Marshal Barnes was a master at maintaining the calm.

On that Monday the main election events began to take place in Judge Sauls's courtroom. The Tuesday morning news reports stated that no fewer than nineteen lawyers were in Judge Sauls's courtroom as Al Gore became the first presidential candidate in history to challenge the results of a certified election.

Our court was busy preparing for and hearing the oral arguments in cases that had nothing to do with the presidential election. In a separate development, Governor Jeb Bush scheduled an execution to be held late in December, which meant that we would also have to focus on that capital case. There are always issues that have to be decided by the court after an execution is scheduled. I thought to myself that Governor Bush must have missed the fact that we were pretty consumed with other matters.

The justices quickly agreed to stay that execution until after the first of the New Year. It was evident that we would have to study and perhaps react to what the U.S. Supreme Court was going to rule in the election case in which that Court had scheduled oral argument on the coming Friday, December 1. We would also, within a short period, have for review not only the case that was then being heard by Judge Sauls, but additionally election cases involving many other issues that were reaching final decisions in various lower courts throughout Florida.

Our oral arguments went on as scheduled beginning at 9:00 a.m. Tuesday morning. At the postargument conference, we had a general discussion of the consolidated butterfly-ballot cases. We did not make a decision on the cases at that time. The final briefs in the case were due to be filed by 4:00 p.m. on Wednesday, and we agreed to have another conference on the cases as soon as practical after all the briefs had been received. There appeared to be preliminary consensus that the form of the ballot did not violate the election statute, and that the circuit court denying relief should be affirmed.

We completed our conference by midafternoon, and I returned to my office. I then worked on the cases scheduled for the next day's oral argument, tended to some court administrative matters, and left for home around 5:00 p.m. I was uncertain when the case being heard by Judge Sauls would reach our court, but I had no doubt it would be very soon.

On my way home, the radio news reports were about developments in Judge Sauls's court. Among Judge Sauls's rulings, he had ordered that the disputed Miami-Dade and Palm Beach Counties' ballots be transported to his courtroom in Tallahassee by police escort. The news reports were that this totaled 14,000 ballots.

Judge Sauls scheduled a hearing to be held Saturday, December 2, 2000, to consider whether the ballots would be counted. Judge Sauls had indicated that the ballots would not necessarily be counted when they arrived. Mr. Boies, who again was representing Gore, had requested Judge Sauls to immediately begin counting the ballots when they arrived in Judge Sauls's court. Judge Sauls denied that request, and it was reported that Mr. Boies had announced that he would file an emergency petition in our court seeking for us to order that the counting begin.

Even though I did not have time to study what was happening in other courts, I knew that numerous other cases pending in both the federal and Florida state courts were being processed, and that more cases were being filed each day. Craig Waters advised me that there were even cases filed in some county courts. This meant that now there were election cases pending in every level of court that had jurisdiction in Florida law.

Still, I was quite certain the main action was the one before Judge Sauls. It was apparent to me that the Gore team had decided to concentrate on that contest. Obviously Gore's counsel now wanted to take advantage of the broad power to correct irregularities provided by the contest statute to a circuit judge. A contest appeared to be Gore's best opportunity to get a continued counting of the ballots. However, it was also apparent that the contest statute gave to a circuit judge reasonable discretion as to what was to be done in the circumstances of a particular contest. Whichever way Judge Sauls ruled in the contest in his court, I was confident that the case would quickly make its way to our court.

While this was going on in the judicial branch, I knew from newspapers that Republican state legislative leaders were exploring whether to call a special legislative session to mandate the state's presidential electors for Bush. The reported plan was for the legislature's Republican majority to select a slate of presidential electors to cast Florida's electoral votes for Bush at the national meeting of the presidential electors if the courts by the date of that meeting had not approved certification of Bush as the winner of the election in Florida. News reports indicated that legislative leaders had received legal advice from their constitutional law experts that this could be done.

I had no doubt that Speaker of the House Tom Feeney was in favor of such legislative action. Speaker Feeney had voiced strong reaction against our decision in the protest case. Moreover, as I have previously stated, the Republican majority in the House, of which Feeney was the leader, had in the recent past been critical of our court's decisions in other matters. In September 2000, a short two months before the election controversy, Speaker Feeney had denounced in very strong terms the court's decision in *Armstrong v. Harris*, which, as I have stated, involved the ballot initiative placed on the 1998 election ballot involving the death penalty. The strong language in the majority opinion in *Armstrong v. Harris*, and Speaker Feeney's equally strong critical reaction to it, were still fresh when the protest case decision issued on November 21, 2000.

I took reports of the legislative special session seriously. I thought it would likely complicate an already full slate of issues. I knew that if the legislature selected its own slate of presidential electors, that would give rise to further legal and political disputes both in courts and Congress. If the legislature chose to mandate a slate of electors, there would not be a final resolution of controversies as to Florida's electors until after December 12, 2000, the safe-harbor date.

On Wednesday, we continued with our regular oral argument schedule, after which we had our usual conference. During conference we were notified by Tom Hall that Gore had filed a petition in our court addressing Judge Sauls's denial of the Gore emergency request to start counting the ballots. The petition asked us either to count the ballots ourselves or require Judge Sauls to speed up the schedule in the contest case. I set a conference for 4:00 p.m. to consider the butterfly-ballot case as well as the Gore petition.

The conference began promptly, and we quickly reached consensus on the butterfly-ballot case. We unanimously concluded that though the ballot form may have been confusing, the form was not in conflict with the election statute, and was within the discretion of the Palm Beach County election supervisor. We agreed to affirm the trial court with an order that dealt only with the form of the ballot, so that the issue of the proper relief in a contest that found there to be defects in a presidential election would not be decided in that case. That issue would await the appeal of Judge Sauls's final ruling in the case he was hearing. Our order did end the litigation over the butterfly ballot.

The discussion of the Gore petition to start the counting of the ballots took much longer than the discussion about the butterfly ballot. There were definite views expressed by some justices that it was urgent that counting be done. I, however, did not see a basis for our court to consider the issue. We did not have an appeal before us in the case.

Ultimately the court decided to deny the petition without prejudice. No member of the court dissented to the order, which was issued after the conference adjourned.

On Friday, December 1, 2000, the case involving our November 21 decision was heard in oral argument at the U.S. Supreme Court. As the days had rolled by and oral argument, in what I thought was a moot case, drew closer and closer, I continued to wonder why a case about the protest phase of the election statute, which was over, and at the end of which the petitioner, Bush, needed no relief since he had been certified the winner of the election, would go forward to a decision. The U.S. Supreme Court proceeding with the case was different from what I had known the Supreme Court to do in other cases. My experience was that the Supreme Court did not decide hypothetical cases in which the petitioner required no relief.

Because of the demands of our oral argument cases, the butterfly-ballot case, and the Gore emergency petition on the counting, I did not during that week have time to review the briefs filed in the case before the U.S. Supreme Court. Tom Hall had provided each justice with copies of those briefs so that when time permitted we could see how the issues were presented to the Supreme Court.

On Saturday, December 2, 2000, the contest action proceeded in Judge Sauls's courtroom on television. I did not watch the broadcast. I wanted to consider the appeal in the usual manner, on a printed transcript of the testimony presented at the hearing, the evidence admitted in the proceedings in the trial court, and briefs submitted to our court. I was concerned that watching the presentation on television would unduly influence my decision making. I was aware that the hearing lasted all day.

The annual holiday parade in Tallahassee was on the evening of December 2. As we did every year we lived in Tallahassee, Linda and I went to see the parade begin at around 6:30 p.m. The parade's route, north to south on Tallahassee's Monroe Street, took the parade in front of the Leon County courthouse. As Linda and I stood at that location to watch the parade, I watched a tired group of lawyers trudge out of the courthouse.

15

United States Supreme Court Remands; Judge Sauls Rules

Monday, December 4, 2000, became another historic day in the continuing controversy. Judge Sauls completed the contest hearing the previous evening. At the end of the hearing, Judge Sauls announced that he would issue a ruling by 2:00 p.m. the next day.

I expected the U.S. Supreme Court to fairly quickly issue a decision in the case in which it had heard argument on December 1, perhaps that Monday. Since I finally had the time that morning, I began my day reading the briefs and transcript of the oral argument in the case before the U.S. Supreme Court. I was immediately struck by how different the arguments made to the U.S. Supreme Court were from the arguments made to the Florida Supreme Court. I knew that the arguments would be different since the focus before the U.S. Supreme Court was necessarily on questions of federal law rather than Florida law. However, I did not expect the argument on behalf of Bush to be as different as it was.

The core of the argument Bush made in his brief to the U.S. Supreme Court concerned Article II, Section 1 of the U.S. Constitution and Title 3, Section 5 of the United States Code regarding the selection of presidential electors. Article II, Section 1 states that executive power shall be vested in a president of the United States and chosen by electors each state shall appoint in such manner as the legislature of the state may direct. This section further provides that Congress may determine the time of "chusing" the electors and the day on which they are to give their votes. Title 3, Section 5 of the United States Code provides that if states provide bylaws enacted prior to the day fixed for the appointment of electors for final determination of any controversy or contest concerning the appointment of all or any of the electors by judicial or other methods or other procedures, such final determination of any controversy or contest shall be conclusive (considered a safe-harbor provision). This provision fixed the date for the 2000 election to be December 12.

I looked back at the Bush brief in our court. This confirmed my recollection that federal constitutional and statutory laws were mentioned only in footnote 15, which was near the end of the brief.

In reading Bush's U.S. Supreme Court brief and in the transcript of the oral argument before that Court, I saw the first mention of the U.S. Supreme Court's 1892 decision titled *McPherson v. Blacker*.[1] The case had not been cited in either the briefs or oral argument in our court. I would later see that *McPherson v. Blacker* was the only case authority referred to in the U.S. Supreme Court's opinion vacating and remanding our decision.

I noted that in the oral argument before the U.S. Supreme Court there was very limited questioning by the justices about the conflicts in Florida's election statutes, and there was no discussion of the separate sections in the Florida election statutes pertaining to protest and contest. This amazed me. The lawyers who were presenting and arguing the case before the U.S. Supreme Court obviously knew that the presidential election controversy had moved on from the protest phase to the completely separate and decisive contest. During the entire week preceding the U.S. Supreme Court oral argument on Friday, Judge Sauls had held daily hearings in the contest case, which these lawyers or their colleagues had attended.

Moreover, I did not understand why there was no discussion about what I thought should have been the dispositive fact, which was that Petitioner Bush, following our court's revised deadline for the county supervisors to report the counties' votes to the state, was certified the winner of the election. Any complaints Bush had about the protests

---

1   146 U.S. 1 (1892).

were moot. Bush simply needed no relief from the U.S. Supreme Court because Bush had not been harmed.

What I also did not understand was why there was no questioning of the argument by Bush's counsel, Theodore Olsen, about the lack of focus in our court's decision on Title 3 U.S.C. Section 5, and the harm that resulted from that lack of focus. Mr. Olsen maintained that this section had been adopted by Congress after the 1876 presidential election for the purpose of avoiding the situation that had arisen in the election between Rutherford B. Hayes and Samuel Tilden, arguing:[2]

> The Florida legislature bought into that Federal scheme and now the Florida Supreme Court, which doesn't have any constitutional authority pursuant to Section 5 to do so, upset that scheme, deprived Florida of the benefit of doing exactly what Congress wanted to have happen under Section 5.

This argument was not in the argument made by Bush's counsel when the case had been heard in our court. When I read his assertion, I questioned in my mind in what way we had "deprived" Florida of the benefit of Section 5 (referring to the safe-harbor provision of the federal statute). As I have noted, the facts were that at the time this argument was made by Mr. Olsen to the U.S. Supreme Court, Bush had already been certified as the winner of the Florida election, which ended the protests, and there was the ongoing contest before Judge Sauls. I did not see how anyone had been deprived of anything at the point in time that the argument was being made. If the contest was finally determined by December 12, 2000, no one would be deprived of any right under Section 5. Whether the contest would be finally resolved by December 12, 2000, of course, was a matter that would be determined in the future and could not be known on December 1, 2000.

However, this comment by Mr. Olsen went unchallenged by the Court. I was beginning to believe that there really was a failure at the U.S. Supreme Court to consider the two-phased procedure in the Florida election statutes for protest and contest.

While I was reading the briefs and puzzling over the transcript of

---

2   Transcript of Oral Argument, Friday, December 1, 2000, 26.

the oral argument, Tom Hall notified me that he had just received a telephone call from the clerk's office at the U.S. Supreme Court that the Supreme Court would issue its decision in the case later that morning. Tom Hall also notified me that Judge Sauls had announced that he would wait until the U.S. Supreme Court issued its opinion before releasing an order in the contest case.

Not too many minutes passed before Tom Hall notified me that the Supreme Court was vacating our decision and remanding the case back to us for further explanation of the basis for our decision. My first thought was that the U.S. Supreme Court had correctly decided not to make a decision in the controversy at this interim stage. Even though it had vacated our decision, the Supreme Court had not made a decision in the case; instead, it had punted.

My second thought was that the Supreme Court's remand was as puzzling as its accepting and reviewing the case at the time and at the point in the controversy when it did. I did not understand why, if the Supreme Court decided only to vacate our decision and not reach a decision of its own, the Supreme Court did not simply hold the case until the end of the ongoing contest case before Judge Sauls. Again, I pondered whether the U.S. Supreme Court had considered Florida's two phases of protest and contest.

Surely, if the U.S. Supreme Court had considered that the controversy was in the contest phase, the Court would have concluded that it would not make sense for us to return to consideration of a case about the protest. To me there simply could be no doubt that what had happened in the protest phase was now only of historic interest or concern. I was convinced that Bush plainly needed no judicial relief by a revision of our remanded opinion.

Judge Sauls was going to rule that afternoon in the contest phase. It was my belief that regardless of the remand of the protest case to us, our court's concentration between the afternoon of December 4 and December 12 had to be directed to reaching a final decision in the contest. This conclusion was not based on any disrespect for the U.S. Supreme Court or any questioning of that Court's ultimate authority. My conclusion was simply based upon the practical dictates of time and capacity.

As I stated earlier, the only case precedent referenced in the Supreme Court's opinion vacating our decision was the 1892 opinion in *McPherson v. Blacker*.[3] I located that opinion and read it. I admit my first impression was disbelief and dismay that the only precedent referred to by the U.S. Supreme Court was over a century old, and was from an era in which the precedent most often referred to was the universally repudiated racial segregation case of *Plessy v. Ferguson*.[4] I was struck by how ironic it was that that the widely criticized *Plessy* Court had decided the binding precedent in a 2000 presidential election case, and involved whether voters in a presidential election have the right to have their votes counted.

I had even more doubt about the citation to that case after I read the *McPherson v. Blacker* opinion. I saw that that decision addressed issues totally different from those we had considered. In that case, the issue was whether the Michigan legislature could adopt a method of selecting electors by congressional districts rather than by statewide selection. In reaching the unremarkable conclusion that the Michigan legislature could do that, the Court stated:[5]

> . . . it is seen that from the formation of the government until now the practical construction of the clause (for selecting electors) has conceded plenary power to the state legislature in the manner of appointment of electors.

The statement concerned a setting so strikingly different from our situation involving the construction of conflicting election statutes that it appeared completely unrelated.

I also thought the context in which the *McPherson* opinion had been referenced by the U.S. Supreme Court was puzzling. The remand opinion set out another quote from *McPherson*:

> [Article II, Section 1, cl 2] does not read that the people or citizens shall appoint, but that each state shall; and if the words "in such manner as the legislature thereof may direct," had been omitted

---

3   *Bush v. Palm Beach County Canvassing Board* 531 U.S. 70; 121 S.Ct. 471 (2000).
4   163 U.S. 537 (1896).
5   146 U.S. at 10 (1892).

it would seem that the legislative power of appointment could have been successfully questioned in the absence of any provision in the state constitution in that regard. Hence, the insertion of those words, while operating as a limitation upon the State in respect of any attempt to circumscribe the legislative power, cannot be held to operate as a limitation on that power itself.[6]

Though that was perhaps interesting to note from the 1890s, in the year 2000 it was hardly a current or material question whether the selection of electors was by direct vote of the voters or by the legislature. In Florida, there had been direct popular election of presidential electors for more than 150 years. No state legislature in any state had chosen presidential electors other than by direct popular election since 1876. The power bestowed by the U.S. Constitution on the Florida legislature had long been ceded to Florida's voters.

The U.S. Supreme Court's remand opinion seemed to indicate that we had erred if we relied on the Florida Constitution's right to vote rather than deferring to the legislature's power in the selection of delegates. The Court said:

> There are expressions in the opinion of the Supreme Court of Florida that may be read to indicate that it construed the Florida Election Code without regard to the extent to which the Florida Constitution could, consistent with Art. II, Section 1, cl 2 "circumscribe legislative power." The opinion states, for example, that "to the extent that the legislature may enact laws regulating the electoral process those laws are valid only if they impose no unreasonable or unnecessary restraints on the right of suffrage guaranteed by the State constitution."[7]

What the U.S. Supreme Court was apparently intending in this passage was difficult for me to accept. This statement seemed at odds with the most fundamental of legal principles that the federal and state constitutions were the bedrock of all laws. Moreover, I failed to understand why the Florida legislature did not have to defer to the Florida

---

6   531 U.S. at 76 (2000).

7   531 U.S. at 77 (2000).

Constitution in the selection of presidential electors, since the legislature was dependent on the Florida Constitution for all its power and, in fact, for its very existence. This was a point long ingrained in Florida law as recognized by our court in 1935 by expressly stating: "The legislature is the creature of the Constitution and can never be superior in powers to the will of the people as written by them in the Constitution" (*Colman, Sheriff v. State*).[8]

Although I had these reservations, I was intent upon honoring the decision of the U.S. Supreme Court on the law in our review of the contest. I knew that the *McPherson* case had to be understood and applied as our court moved forward in the contest case. As I earlier noted, I respected the U.S. Supreme Court as the ultimate court of last resort.

Upon receiving the U.S. Supreme Court decision, I scheduled a conference for that afternoon to discuss how the court should proceed now that our decision had been remanded to us. We had a long discussion. Several members of the court wanted to immediately turn attention to the U.S. Supreme Court's remand and quickly issue a new opinion in that case. Even following the long discussion, I did not agree. I continued to steadfastly believe that our concentration had to be on the contest case. I knew it was necessary to get the contest case heard in our court at as early a time as possible if that case, and through it the presidential controversy, was to be finally decided by the safe-harbor date of December 12, 2000.

By the end of the court's conference, the justices agreed that the remand opinion needed to be thoroughly analyzed, and that we should get input from counsel for the parties before deciding how to proceed. We ordered briefs to be submitted to us the next day. While we were in that conference, Tom Hall advised that Judge Sauls had ruled and denied relief to Gore.

With that word, all of the justices also agreed that the appeal in Judge Sauls's case had to be the priority for our court. The result of Judge Sauls's ruling meant that the manual counting of the ballots that he had ordered be delivered to his court would not be done. Several justices reacted angrily to the fact that Judge Sauls would not have the

---

8   159 So.504 (Fla. 1935).

votes then present in his courtroom counted and wanted our court to issue an order to immediately start manually counting the votes. After another long and emotional discussion, in which it was apparent that the court was divided as to whether or not to order manual counting, the result was that no order was issued to begin the counting of the ballots. We agreed to adjourn the conference until 10:00 a.m. the next day.

I returned to my office and read Judge Sauls's order.[9] Oral argument needed to be set as soon as practical. I had Craig Waters come to my office, and we worked out a tentative schedule to have oral argument in the case on that coming Thursday, December 7, 2000. I would present the suggested schedule to the justices at the conference the next morning. We would then send out the notices, immediately endeavoring to expend every effort to finalize the decision within the safe-harbor time period.

---

9   Final Judgment Case cv00-2808, Circuit Court Leon County.

16

Our Court Reviews Judge Sauls's Order: Decision and Division

As expected, the pass-through of Judge Sauls's order came from the First District Court of Appeals late on the evening of December 4. On December 5, we began our conference at 10:00 a.m. The tension among the justices, which had been increasing in the conference the day before, was ratcheted up even more as this conference began. The conference was all business, with none of the lighthearted chatter that was usually part of the interaction among the justices. The statements by the justices were direct and terse. With each passing hour, the chances of successfully counting the contested ballots were slipping away. This made some of the justices more and more eager for the court to do something.

There was again a discussion about whether our court should immediately order the counting of the more than 9,000 Miami-Dade County votes that the county canvassing board had indicated were not counted by machine counting. These ballots were not reviewed when the county canvassing board decided on November 22, 2000, to stop counting. I continued to oppose entering an order requiring counting at that time. My view was that the court needed to review Judge Sauls's decision, and hear the parties' arguments about that decision before ruling on counting the ballots. Our court issuing an order on whether the ballots should be counted would be ruling on Judge Sauls's decision not to count the ballots.

I recognized that not ruling at that time on the counting issue also could result in there being no more counting. Time was running out. I understood that reality.

I had agreed with our court's orders in which, before hearing and deciding the protest case, we had allowed counting to continue over Bush's objection. However, I considered the earlier situation to be different. In the earlier situation, counting was ongoing when Secretary Harris ordered it to end. The reverse was now true. Judge Sauls had decided not to count. The situation now required us to determine the merits of Judge Sauls's decision before ordering that counting should be renewed.

I also thought that before our court made any further decisions, we had to come to grips with the *McPherson v. Blacker* decision, since the U.S. Supreme Court had called that decision to our attention in its remand order. I was concerned about whether the *McPherson* decision could be read to mean that our court did not have a role in an election contest. The statute authorizing the contest referred only to the circuit court, and was silent as to a right to appeal to an appellate court. The U.S. Supreme Court had expressly set out the part of the *McPherson* opinion that said that the legislature had "plenary power" in the selection of presidential electors. *Webster's New World Dictionary* defines "plenary" to mean "full, complete, and absolute." I accepted that our court had to respect this legislative power.

I thought the proper course was for our court to expedite the review of Judge Sauls's order. Following another long discussion covering the same ground about time running out for manual counting, this was the course that prevailed, and the expedited oral argument in the contest case was scheduled for 10:00 a.m. on December 7, 2000, in less than forty-eight hours. I knew that the time might not be the best for the television networks, with whom we were continuing to coordinate court proceedings so that our decision making would be seen by as many viewers as possible. But we had no choice but to hear the arguments at that time.

After the discussion of the contest case, we briefly returned to consideration of the U.S. Supreme Court opinion in the remand. I asked one of the justices to have staff develop an opinion responding to the remand. I continued to believe that the case involving the protest should not take priority over the justices' preparation for oral argument and consideration of Judge Sauls's order. On the morning of December 6, 2000, I received a draft opinion responding to the remand. I thought the draft needed further work. I put it aside and returned to concentrating on the contest case.

I first reviewed in detail Judge Sauls's Order.[1] The order contained many separate rulings. Foremost, Judge Sauls had reached the conclusion that in order for Gore to prevail in a contest of ballots in a particular county, there had to be a reasonable probability that, but for the irregularity or inaccuracy of the ballots, the statewide results of the election, not just the particular county's results, would have been different. This meant that the statewide result of the election would have to have been different from that certified by the State Election Commission on November 26, 2000. Judge Sauls held that the preponderance of evidence presented in the case before him failed to show that the statewide outcome of the election would have been different.

Judge Sauls said in his order that the evidence did not establish any illegality, dishonesty, gross negligence, improper influence, coercion, or fraud in the balloting or counting processes. Judge Sauls held that none of the county canvassing boards had abused their discretion in the processing or counting of the ballots. Judge Sauls stated that in order to prevail, Gore would have to place at issue, and seek as a remedy, a review and recount of all ballots in all Florida counties. Judge Sauls ruled that Gore had failed to present a sufficient legal basis upon which to move forward to a review and counting of the ballots that had been transported to his courtroom.

Judge Sauls's order was a sweeping and complete victory for Bush.

I next turned to Gore's brief. Gore, of course, attacked Judge Sauls's order on all issues. Gore maintained that his burden pursuant to Florida Statute 102.168 was only to show that the counts in Miami-Dade and Palm Beach Counties did not include a number of "legal votes," and that

---

1   Final Judgment Case cv00-2808, Circuit Court Leon County; Findings and Conclusions in the transcript attached to the Final Judgment.

this was sufficient for him to succeed in having the votes counted. Gore asserted that Judge Sauls's refusal to examine more than 9,000 votes from Miami-Dade County and 3,300 votes from Palm Beach County was plainly in error. Gore argued that Judge Sauls's decision rested on three flawed conclusions of law: (1) that a court in an election contest may not review only the contested ballots, but rather must review all ballots cast for the office; (2) that the issue in a contest action is not whether the county canvassing board abused its discretion; and (3) that the party bringing the contest must establish a reasonable probability that the results of the election would have been changed before the court may review the ballots.

Bush and Secretary Harris each filed briefs that essentially argued that Judge Sauls was correct in each of the conclusions and holdings in the order.

My initial conclusion from my review of Judge Sauls's order and the briefs was that Judge Sauls's reasoning did have flaws, especially as to the issue of whether he should have examined the ballots that he had ordered be transported to his courtroom. Once the ballots were in his Tallahassee courtroom, I thought it naturally followed that the ballots should have been counted. I thought he erred in refusing to account for the undisputed fact that before the Miami-Dade Canvassing Board had decided to stop counting on November 22, 2000, there had been legal votes identified that were not included in the certified count. It appeared from the evidence that this would have resulted in a net increase in the Gore vote of 168 votes.

However, my main focus at that time was reaching a conclusion about the proper role of our court at this stage of the election controversy. It was December 5, 2000, and, as our court had determined, the earliest we could reasonably and fairly have oral argument was December 7, 2000. The deadline to meet the safe-harbor provision was December 12, 2000.

I believed strongly that coming within the safe-harbor provision was exceedingly important not only to Florida's voters, but to the nation. I thought that the alternative of continuing the controversy after the safe-harbor date would only create confusion and chaos. I foresaw a long period in which the transfer of power would hang in the balance.

Moreover, we had a ruling from the trial judge denying Gore relief under the contest statute. Though I continued to believe our November 21 decision had been correct, I knew that responsibility for the present time crunch rested on our extension of the time for the protest phase.

I was notified during the morning of December 6, 2000, that the legislative leaders of the Florida House and Senate had called the special session to begin at noon on December 8, 2000. The report noted that the House and Senate intended to name a slate of twenty-five electors on December 13, 2000, which would be after the expiration of the safe-harbor date and would only proceed if the judicial matters had not been resolved by then.

On December 7, 2000, at 9:45 a.m., the justices again gathered in the conference room behind the courtroom. The mood in the conference room was noticeably much more tense than the mood had been before the oral argument on November 20, 2000, in the protest case. I knew the pressure level reflected the fact that we had reached the climactic point in the controversy, and that the justices all thought our court would be seriously divided in the decision in the contest. The divisions were evident not only in the stated words, but in the tone and strong disagreements in the discussions we had had on Gore's emergency motion to count the ballots. I had also picked up from my law clerks that the common chatter that is usual among clerks about cases being heard by the court was muted and strained.

In the oral argument, Mr. Boies again spoke for Gore, Mr. Richard for Bush, and Mr. Klock for Secretary Harris. The courtroom was once again filled to capacity. I opened with a question about the *McPherson v. Blacker* case. I wanted counsel to state their positions on the application of that case in our present review. I pointed out that it was the only case authority referred to in the U.S. Supreme Court remand to us, and that it was authority that had not been cited to us when the case was previously before us for review. I asked the lawyers if they thought our court had a role at all in the contest. Each seemed surprised by my question and quickly answered that our court did have a role.

I was a little surprised that that was Mr. Richard's answer. I thought Mr. Richard's answer would likely be that, since the statute referred only to the circuit court's jurisdiction, an appeal was not statutorily authorized. I understood, however, that he had not thought through the consequences of such an answer. The natural response to my question that Mr. Richard gave was that there was always a right to appeal a circuit judge's decision, and that in this instance the right to appeal was implicit in the statute. I also recognized that Mr. Boies did not want to spend much time on the question. His answer was yes, and he did not elaborate. No other member of our court asked any questions about this, and the argument quickly moved to other subjects.

This oral argument was only about half as long as the first oral argument. I could tell early into the argument that there was a majority of the justices determined to reverse Judge Sauls's decision. There were a number of very skeptical questions about the standard Judge Sauls had used in determining that the ballots should not be counted. It was apparent that a majority of the justices did not think that the issue had been correctly resolved by application of an abuse-of-discretion standard to the decisions of the county canvassing boards. The most troubling questions to me, however, were those posed by Justice Lewis, which indicated he was considering ordering a recount of votes in every county. My heart sank. That could not realistically and reliably be done within the time remaining during the safe-harbor period. Then, when Justice Pariente followed Justice Lewis with a similar question, I knew we were headed for trouble.

Based upon his argument, I concluded that Mr. Boies agreed with my conclusion that a statewide recount would be a problem. In fact, Mr. Boies argued that Judge Sauls had erred when he held that the remedy, if granted in a presidential election, had to be determined on the basis of whether the statewide result would have been different.

The oral argument was completed, and we were back in the conference room by 11:30 a.m. We went around the table to see how each justice was leaning in the case. This confirmed that we were split with a majority in favor of reversing Judge Sauls, but we still had intense discussion about various issues. I decided that we should break for lunch. Each justice needed time to contemplate his or her decision. We returned to the conference room around 3:00 p.m. We had more discussion of our individual positions for about another two hours. At times the discussions became heated, although very little anger was displayed. Around 5:00 p.m., I concluded that we were not going to complete our discussions that night, so we ended the conference and scheduled to begin again at 10:00 a.m. the next morning, December 8, 2000. All the justices were committed to rendering a decision by the end of that day.

I went to my office and met with my staff lawyers. I had come to the conclusion that it was time to end the Florida presidential election controversy. I knew that this was not going to be the majority view of the justices, and that I would have to write a dissent. I explained to my staff lawyers what I had concluded. My staff was very aware that this was likely going to happen and wanted to go directly to work on the dissent. I assigned them to work on specific issues and the drafting of a dissent.

I returned to the court before 6:00 a.m. My staff had worked almost the entire night on the assignments I had given them. Using the staff's work, I then began to hand-write my dissent. Although by this time I had become comfortable with writing on the computer, I still preferred to hand-write drafts of opinions. I found that I could conceptualize better by writing out my thoughts.

I was advised by my staff that several of the justices were already in their offices, and soon thereafter I began receiving their opinions. I noted that there continued to be a majority of justices for reversing Judge Sauls, but I did not find a majority supporting a statewide recount. I learned that there were ongoing discussions among the justices about an appropriate course of action. Several justices asked that I postpone the 10:00 a.m. conference. We finally gathered in the conference room at 1:15 p.m. In this conference there was nothing to discuss. The division between the majority and the dissenting justices plainly could not be bridged. I quickly left so that the majority could discuss their opinion without me.

About 2:15 p.m., I was notified that a majority of four votes—Justices Anstead, Pariente, Lewis, and Quince—which was the majority when the decision issued, had agreed to reverse Judge Sauls's decision not to count the Miami-Dade ballots and to hold that the Circuit Court of Leon County had authority to order the supervisors of elections and county canvassing boards in all counties that had not conducted a manual recount of undervotes (ballots in which the machine counting did not record a vote for president) to do so. I understood that what the majority was ordering meant a statewide counting of votes.

I knew that there would be an immediate adverse reaction by the Florida legislature.

I thought it was doubtful that practical logistics would allow there to be completed within a period of a few days a manual recount of undervoted ballots in a good many of the counties. There were just too many practical problems. The ballots were undoubtedly stored, and they would have to be taken out of storage, and then painstakingly researched for undervotes. This could take weeks, not days. The recounts would then spawn additional controversies that would have to be resolved. We were back full circle to the problem of there not being standards for the manual counting of votes included in the election statutes. Clearly this statewide recount could not be finally concluded by December 12, 2000.

Overlaying all of the practical problems was my realization that regardless of how much more counting was done, or what was eventually ordered by our court or by the U.S. Supreme Court, or done by the Florida legislature or Congress, there would not be any more certainty of the correctness of the vote count. At this point I concluded that after all the counting was done, the margin of error was always going to be greater than the margin of victory.

I felt in all my being that what the majority was about to do was wrong. I wanted badly to find some way to find a fourth vote to obtain a different majority, affirm Judge Sauls, and end the case. Yet I knew that I was powerless to do this. For the first time in the days since the election, I was depressed, shaken, and actually fearful about what was about to happen, and how the controversy would move forward. I wanted to go out to the steps of the Supreme Court Building where Craig Waters reported the court's actions and shout my fears, frustrations, and concerns. But of course I knew I could not do that. My only course was to explain my deep-seated feelings as plainly as I could in a dissenting opinion. My hope had to be that I could explain the situation with sufficient clarity and alarm that the U.S. Supreme Court would again come into the case. I was by no means certain that would happen. In part I wrote:

> My succinct conclusion is that the majority's decision to return the case to the circuit court for a count of the under votes either from Miami-Dade County or all the counties has no foundation in the law of Florida as it existed on November 7, 2000 or any time until the issuance of this opinion. The majority returns the case to the circuit court for this partial recount of under votes on the basis of unknown, or at best, ambiguous standards with authority to obtain help from others, the credentials, qualifications and objectivity of whom are totally unknown. That is but a first glance at the imponderable problems the majority creates.
>
> Importantly to me, I have a deep and abiding concern that the prolonging of judicial process in this counting contest propels this country and this state into an unprecedented and unnecessary constitutional crisis. I have to conclude that there is a real and present likelihood that this constitutional crisis will do substantial damage to our country, our state and to this court as an institution.
>
> This court's responsibility must be to balance the contest allegations against the rights of all Florida voters who are not involved in contests to have their votes counted in the Electoral College. To me, it is inescapable that there is no practical way for the contest to continue for the good of this country and this state.
>
> This case has reached the point where finality must take precedence over continued judicial process.

I had the dissent finalized and circulated it to the other justices.

I received Justice Harding's dissent, which was written in less strident language than mine. Not long after that, I received Justice Shaw's vote concurring in Justice Harding's dissent. I likewise concurred in Justice Harding's dissent. Thus, Justice Harding and I each had dissenting opinions published when the majority opinion was released. However, we could not get a fourth vote to join our dissents.

The majority opinion was received with the four justices concurring in it, and the remainder of the afternoon was spent with the court staff editing all of the opinions. I was most concerned about the majority ordering a statewide recount, which I was absolutely certain could not be effectively accomplished by the safe-harbor date of December 12, 2000. Finally, at 6:30 p.m., all opinions were ready to be released.[2] Craig Waters announced the decision from the steps of the Supreme Court Building.

After the court's decision was released, the media almost immediately expressed a lot of disbelief and shock. Judge Sauls, to whom the majority had remanded the case for the additional proceedings, immediately announced that he was removing himself from the case.

Circuit Judge Terry Lewis, the same trial judge whose order our court had reversed in the protest case, was assigned the case. Judge Lewis scheduled an immediate hearing to discuss how to proceed.[3]

---

2   772 So.2d 1243 (Fla. 2000).

3   772 So.2d at 1261 (Fla. 2000), majority opinion directed: "nor can we ignore the correctness of the assertions that any analysis and ultimate remedy should be made on a statewide basis."

17

The Supremes End the Tale

The media reports on December 9, 2000, focused on the split decision and the stunning opinion of the majority. Following the issuance of our court's decision during the night of December 8, Circuit Judge Lewis convened a hearing and heard argument by counsel for the parties for two hours as to how to proceed. He then spent another two hours working out a procedure for the recounting. His decision was to order the counting of the 9,000 Miami-Dade ballots to begin at 8:00 a.m. on December 9, 2000, at the Leon County Public Library and the recounting of the undervoted ballots in the other counties to be conducted by the county canvassing boards. The county canvassing boards were to report to him their plans for the recounting by noon on December 9, 2000, and to complete their recounting by 2:00 p.m. on December 10, 2000. Judge Lewis was certainly trying his best. As appropriate for an exceptionally good former basketball player, which I knew from personal experience he was, Judge Lewis put on a full-court press.

However, almost immediately on December 9, 2000, nearly every county reported significant problems as they attempted to count the ballots. County election supervisors took different directions, workers argued about what to do and how to do it, and some refused to do anything. Some counties, large and small, did not have software to sort out the ballots that had the undervotes. It was reported, for example, that Orange County (Orlando) would have to sort through 282,500 ballots to locate 966 undervotes. Four counties refused to do the ordered sorting and counting. Many counties reported that there were a substantial number of overvoted ballots (ballots in which there were indications of a vote for more than one presidential candidate).[1]

There was a report that Bush had filed a petition in both the U.S. Supreme Court and the U.S. Court of Appeals for the Eleventh Circuit to halt the counting. Additionally, Bush petitioned the U.S. Supreme Court to review our court's decision.

Since the case was now out of our court, and the pressure relieved at least temporarily, Linda and I went to Governor's Square Mall in Tallahassee to do some Christmas shopping. While there, we had lunch in a restaurant where we saw my former colleague Ben Overton. He asked whether we had heard that morning from the U.S. Supreme Court in response to Bush's filings in that court. I said I had not. Former Justice Overton just shook his head, which I took to mean that he thought the matter was in a very confused state.

Just as Linda and I returned home in the early afternoon, Craig Waters called my cell phone to tell me that the U.S. Supreme Court, in a 5–4 vote, had stayed the counting, agreed to review our court's December 8 decision, and scheduled oral argument for Monday, December 11, 2000.[2] As the old slogan says, "I had that feeling of *relief*."

I immediately went to the court to read the U.S. Supreme Court's order. I asked Tom Hall to make certain that Circuit Judge Lewis had a copy of the stay order. I knew that he had already made certain that the other justices had a copy of the order. Tom Hall then spoke by telephone with the clerk's office at the U.S. Supreme Court to determine the records the Supreme Court wanted transmitted to Washington. Marshal Barnes made arrangements with the Florida Highway Patrol to fly Tom Hall to Washington to deliver that portion of the court record sought by the Supreme Court. There was no reason to convene our court on that Saturday afternoon so I did not seek to have the justices come to the court or have a telephone conference. I felt this was the correct way to proceed since I well knew that those in the majority felt as strongly about the correctness of their decision as I did about my dissent, and

---

1   "Court Ordered Recount Was a Guessing Game," *Orlando Sentinel*, November 12, 2011.

2   531 U.S. 1046; 121 S.Ct. 512.

that the U.S. Supreme Court's stay order would be very frustrating to them.

On Monday morning, December 11, 2000, I sent notice to the other justices that we would have a conference that afternoon at 2:00 p.m. to consider other presidential election cases that were forwarded to our court. These included cases from various circuits around Florida in which the courts had decided cases involving various issues as to absentee ballots.

Before 2:00 p.m., an audio recording of the morning's oral argument at the U.S. Supreme Court arrived, and several justices, including me, listened to that audio. During the oral argument, Justice Sandra Day O'Connor criticized our court for not responding to the remand in the protest case. As the conference began, the mood was very tense. There was no discussion of the U.S. Supreme Court's stay order or of it taking the contest case. However, all of the justices, except me, wanted to issue that afternoon a revised opinion in the protest case. A discussion of the revised opinion took the entire conference.

I did not agree to issuing at that time an opinion that revised our November 21, 2000, opinion. Even though I had great respect for and was an admirer of Justice O'Connor, I was opposed to issuing an immediate opinion. I was concerned that another opinion about counting would only further confuse the situation. Moreover, what we said at this point about the protest could only be academic. The other justices were unmoved by my disagreement. I assumed some of the justices thought that immediately getting out a revised opinion in the protest case would cause the Supreme Court to look more favorably on the court's majority opinion in the contest case, which the Supreme Court was then considering.

A new draft opinion was circulated soon after the conference, to which I was the lone dissenter. I dissented not only because I was opposed to the timing of issuing the opinion; I also dissented because the new opinion indicated that we had not relied upon the state constitution in our decision when, in fact, I believed that we had. It would have been illogical for us not to have done so.

We had another conference on the morning of December 12, 2000, to discuss other election cases. We did make decisions in many of those cases. But I had no doubt that the primary thoughts in every justice's mind were about the review pending before the Supreme Court. With the passage of each hour, I thought the chances of the Supreme Court affirming the majority opinion in the contest case were growing smaller. To again begin the counting of ballots on the safe-harbor date made no sense. Yet of course there could be no certainty until the Supreme Court issued its decision.

On the evening of December 12, 2000, Linda and I went to a restaurant for dinner and then attended a traveling Broadway show at the Tallahassee Civic Center. At the intermission I told Linda that I could not sit through the rest of the performance. All of my thoughts were consumed by when the Supreme Court would rule. Shortly after we arrived home, there was a television report that the Supreme Court had reached a decision, and that it would be released in a few minutes, which would be close to 10:00 p.m.

The network reporter came on a few minutes later and announced that the case was being remanded back to us. My heart pounded! Linda shouted, "Why would they do that???" Like Linda, I had no idea what we could do upon remand. Blessedly, a few minutes later the reporter corrected the remand report, and said that, by a vote of 5–4, the U.S. Supreme Court had reversed our court's majority opinion. Linda and I both calmed down. About that time Tom Hall called and said that the clerk of the Supreme Court was e-mailing the opinion to him. Tom called back shortly and read the Court's majority opinion to me.[3] Even after the reading by Tom, I was still uncertain if there was anything left for our court to do.

I slept little that night and went to the court very early the next morning. I read the opinions of the Supreme Court and was convinced that there was nothing further for our court to do. Shortly after 11:00 a.m., Craig Waters notified me that Gore was going to concede.

The 2000 Florida presidential election controversy was *final*. Florida's electors could vote in the Electoral College when it met to vote for president on December 18, 2000. There was basically silence in the hallways of our court. I think that this evidenced the divisions that were

---

3   *Bush v. Gore* 531 U.S. 98; 121 S.Ct. 525 (2000).

apparent in the court's December 8, 2000, opinion, and also evidenced *relief* that the controversy was over in our court.

As quickly as they had appeared, the media tents on the steps of the Capitol Building and the blocks of TV satellite trucks disappeared. The crowds and microphones were gone. The year 2000 pre-Christmas festivities at the Florida Supreme Court were concluded. *Bush v. Gore* was history, and the commentaries and critiques of what occurred during those thirty-six days began.

Summation

I turn now to this summation after having, in the course of writing this book, relived the thirty-six days from November 7, 2000, through December 12, 2000, together with the advantage of more than a decade of hindsight, and with the benefit of having read the countless commentaries in articles and books about the decisions of our court and of the U.S. Supreme Court. I have been greatly interested in the commentaries and analysis of the numerous scholars, journalists, media commentators, and politicians who have written and commented. Not unexpectedly, I have agreed with some and disagreed with others.

I have not set out an analysis of the second opinion of the U.S. Supreme Court, which has been the subject of so much of the commentary and analysis, because I agree with the important caveat in the majority's opinion in that decision. The U.S. Supreme Court's opinion stated that it was limited to the then present circumstances. I accept that the decision of a majority of the Supreme Court was vital because of what it did and not because of the reasons or analysis that the majority of that Court gave for its decision. It was at the time, and continues through this writing, to be my firm belief that when the U.S. Supreme Court issued that decision, it was necessary to bring finality to the election controversy, and to avert a governmental crisis that had the potential to be substantial and long-lasting.

At the time of that decision, continuing the controversy served no purpose. In reality, it was improbable that continuing the legal process would have provided any more clarity in determining reliably the actual number of votes that separated Governor Bush and Vice President

Gore. By December 12, 2000, the legal process had established, in the various efforts to resolve the legal issues, that the voting on Election Day, including the absentee votes, was so close, the form of the ballots so defective, and the election statutes such a mess that a more reliable determining of a winner was not reasonably probable regardless of how long the attempts at further counting continued.

I recognize that after the U.S. Supreme Court's decision on December 12, 2000, and Vice President Gore's concession the following morning, there were recounts of Florida's votes that resulted in Gore having more votes than Bush. In early January 2001, national and Florida news media organizations contracted with the National Opinion Research Center at the University of Chicago to build an extensive record of approximately 175,000 rejected and uncertified ballots from the Florida 2000 presidential election. Nine different scenarios were employed to count the ballots. I respect this work.[1] It is my conclusion after examining this extensive work that these after-the-fact recounts confirm the core problem I came to believe existed when the statewide recounts were ordered by our court on December 8, 2000, which was that sufficient standards did not exist for the manual counting of the punch-card ballots in Florida's election statutes on the day of the election. The voting results varied within a narrow range depending on what standards were used.

In the certified vote, Bush was the winner by 537 votes. The newspaper consortium's nine other different scenarios for counting the ballots resulted in Gore having the most votes in five and Bush having the most votes in four. In the scenario following literally the order of our court on December 8, 2000, according to the news media consortium, Bush would have won by 1,720 votes. However, Gore would have won by 107 votes using a scenario that was considered by the news media consortium as the most inclusive statewide scenario, which would have included both what were referred to as undervotes and overvotes. (Undervotes, as noted earlier, were ballots in which no presidential

---

1   National Opinion Research Center at the University of Chicago, published in "Exposing the Flaws," *Orlando Sentinel*, November 12, 2001.

candidate was read by the vote counting machines as having been cast, and overvotes were ballots that were not read by the counting machines because more than one presidential candidate was selected.)

As I observed earlier, this was a story about the transfer of power in the world's most powerful nation. I believe the transfers of power in various parts of the world since 2000 have proven over and over again the benefit and wisdom of our country's citizens' support for and allegiance to the rule of law enforced by an independent court system. Unlike what we have witnessed in the Middle East and in parts of Africa, there was never in the year 2000 any real threat that the disputes surrounding the presidential election would be settled in the streets rather than in the courts.

There was general acceptance throughout the thirty-six days that once the final decision had been made by the final court, power would transfer peacefully. I have often remarked that a striking fact of which we as Americans can and should be proud, and for which we must be grateful, is that the blocks of trucks parked for those thirty-six days across from our court had television transmitters on their roofs, not machine guns. Security in our court, and in front of our court, was never a real issue.

In the more than two-hundred-year history of our country, our citizens have developed an expectation that when a dispute arises that cannot be otherwise worked out, it is the role of the courts to make a decision to end the dispute, and that the decision will be honored and respected. This expectation has grown out of faith on the part of our citizens that courts will provide due process in the presentation and consideration of the dispute, and that the courts will reach a "final" decision with competence, diligence, and without delay. Regardless of the final result of *Bush v. Gore*, or the result of interim decisions during the thirty-six days, I believe that the record demonstrates that both the federal and Florida courts provided due process within the time constraints that had long before the 2000 election been placed by Congress on the resolution of disputes in presidential elections. I also believe that the record demonstrates that the courts reached their decisions with competence, diligence, and without delay.

I have certainly heard, read, and understand the criticisms that have been made by many commentators directed at the decisions made both by the Florida Supreme Court and the U.S. Supreme Court in the processing of the presidential election cases. Not only do I understand the criticism of the courts, but I believe that such criticism is necessary and vital to the proper functioning of the courts. The courts in our country must be independent, but not above criticism. Courts are human, political institutions and must be held accountable by the citizens whom the courts are intended to serve. After all, the courts belong to the citizens, not to the lawyers or the judges who have the privilege to serve in them. Throughout the history of the United States of America, court decisions have been criticized, especially by those who do not agree with various opinions of the court. This has been true since the days of Chief Justice John Marshall and President Thomas Jefferson, through the Civil War, through the Great Depression, through the civil rights and civil liberties cases of the U.S. Supreme Court headed by Chief Justice Earl Warren, through *Bush v. Gore*, and right up to the present date.

As the criticism of the *Bush v. Gore* cases points out, there are without question steps along the way that could have and should have been done differently and better. Hopefully, if the courts are brought in to resolve disputes involving another presidential election, our experience in 2000 will serve to improve the courts' processing of the disputes.

I also believe, however, that it is crucial in a disputed presidential election that the issues be expeditiously processed, and that an early final resolution of the dispute be reached. Resolution by courts will never be as satisfactory as prevention of the basis for disputes by repeated and substantive review and revision of election procedures. The problems that were apparent in the Florida election procedures in 2000 should be reviewed before every presidential election to measure present procedures.

The controversy and disputes in the 2000 presidential election in Florida centered upon preventable problems. Election mechanics and procedures need to be constantly scrutinized and tested so as to forecast and avoid as many problems as reasonably possible. As fundamental as any problem in the *Bush v. Gore* election was the use of the punch-card ballots in more than twenty counties in Florida. The chad problem inherent in these ballots was widely known before the 2000 election. Chads had already been the subject of litigation in several states.

The natural defects in the punch-card ballots grew into what could have become a national disaster because Florida's election statutes, when applied in a presidential election, were a mess. What turned out to be a crucial statutory mistake was to provide authorization for the county canvassing boards to conduct manual recounts, but to provide no standards for that counting. The lack of review and failure to correct conflicts between the sections resulted in confusion and distrust, and consequently led to judicial attempts to fill in legislative blanks.

Issues in the Florida election were also aggravated and complicated by the fact that the secretary of state, who was the most directly involved state administrator, had been active in Bush's Florida presidential campaign, and the attorney general, who is the state's chief legal officer, had been active in the Gore campaign. These offices require nonpartisan objectivity in both appearance and action. The differing legal opinions coming from those offices slowed down the work of tabulating the ballots when time was of the essence. It would have enhanced citizens' confidence and the working of the elections if these officials had not been personally involved in the presidential campaigns.

These were problems that could easily have been remedied before the election, but could not be adequately remedied by the courts after the elections. The proper reach of judicial power does not include revising election statutes or the ballots after an election.

In a paper titled "Counts, Recounts and Election Contest," presented at a 2001 symposium on *Bush v. Gore* at Florida State College of Law, Steve Bickerstaff wrote that the 2000 Florida presidential election was not an event, but a process.[2] I think that thought is very helpful because it is accurate. It was a process through which the election could be sifted and a final decision vital to the transfer of power could be and was made. November 7, 2000, Election Day, began a process stream that

---

2   *Florida State University Law Review* 29, no. 2 (2001), *Bush v. Gore* issue.

flowed from day to day, decision to decision, in largely uncharted territory that had not been contemplated or adequately addressed in the election laws or by election administrators before the election.

The ultimate role of courts is to resolve disputes. That is what the courts did accomplish in *Bush v. Gore*. Through the courts, Americans accomplished settling the transfer of the power of the presidency of the United States without any real fear that the television antennas on the trucks parked across from our court would be changed to guns.

Index

Absentee ballots, 47; *Beckstrom v. Volusia County*, 24; Bush, G. W., and, 2; overseas ballots as, 13–15, 14n1

Allen v. Butterworth, 11, 19

Anstead, Harry, 17; background of, 19–20; liberal label for, 20

Armey, Dick, 93

Armstrong v. Harris, 21–22; as death penalty case, 11–12; Feeney against, 105–6; Shaw on, 18–19

Askew, Reubin, 7, 23

Baker, James, 75, 93

Barnes, Wilson, 24; background of, 25–26; crowd control by, 27, 59, 103; information from, 91; security by, 85, 94, 102–3

Beckstrom v. Volusia County, 24

Bickerstaff, Steve, 135

Boies, David, 70; on contest, 76–77; on deadlines, 77–78, 83–84; oral argument of, 76–78, 83–84, 120–21; Sauls related to, 104

Bowden, Bobby, 62, 62n1

Breyer, Stephen, 10

Briefing schedule, 60

Briefs, 72–73

Broward County Canvassing Board, 73, 76

Buchanan, Patrick, 102

Burton, Judge, 35

Bush, George W.: absentee ballots and, 2; brief of, 72–73; election win for, 2, 99–101; Florida election statutes and, 72–73; lawyers of, 71; Middlebrooks against, 29–30; Panhandle for, 1; petitions from, 127; strategy of, 63; U.S. Supreme Court for, 98–100; votes ahead for, 2

Bush, Jeb, ix–x, 22, 103

Butterfly ballots, 47; appeal on, 102, 106; media on, 13

Butterworth, Bob: *Allen v. Butterworth*, 11, 19; argument of, 70–71; Harris compared to, 35; political affiliations of, 34, 135. *See also* Harris, Katherine

Carroll, Hunter, 13–14

Carvin, Michael, 71; oral argument of, 80–82, 85

Chads, 66; in recounts, 28, 28n1, 48, 67, 78, 97–98, 134–35

Chiles, Lawton: campaign work for, 7–8; in judicial appointment, 8–9

Christopher, Warren, 74

Civil law: in employment, 9; judicial perspective in, 17

Collins, LeRoy, ix–x, 6

Confidentiality, 4

Conservative label, 17

Constitution, U.S.: on electors, 68, 108–9, 113, 124; Florida Constitution compared to, 18

Contest, 109–11, 114; Boies on, 76–77; deadlines and, 90; for Sauls, 101–3, 107–8

Contest of election: Bickerstaff on, 135–36; criticism of, 109–10; Florida election statutes on, 32, 69–70, 76–77; by Gore, 101–2, 104–5. *See also* Harris, Katherine

"Counts, Recounts and Election Contest," (Bickerstaff), 135–36

Criminal law: Florida Supreme Court and, 9–10; judicial perspective in, 17. *See also* Death-penalty cases

Criticism: of contest of election, 109–10; of Florida Supreme Court, 110, 128, 134; of judicial system, 134; of opinion, 93–95; of Sauls's order, 118–19, 121–22; of U.S. Supreme Court, 134

Crowd control, 26; by Barnes, 27, 59, 103; Jackson and, 103; by Waters, 27

D'Alemberte, "Sandy," 62

Deadlines: Boies on, 77–78, 83–84; briefing schedule, 60; contests and, 90; election statutes on, 30–31; for Electoral College, 36, 63, 76; extension of, 88–91; Florida election statutes on, 23–24, 30–31; from Hancock, 76; from Harris, 30, 34, 85; impossibility of, 31–32; for resolution, 2–3; for returns, 65, 88–89; safe harbor, 68–69, 119

Death-penalty cases, 103; cruel and unusual punishment in, 10; Florida Constitution and, 11–12; in Florida Supreme Court, 9–12. See also *Armstrong v. Harris*

Death Penalty Reform Act: Florida Constitution and, 11; postconviction rules for, 35

Delay, Tom, 93

Democratic Party, x; campaign work

in, 6–7; members of, 6, 44. *See also specific Democrats*

Dexter, Douglass, 70

Dissent: from Florida Supreme Court, 3–4, 12, 122–24; from Harding, 124; on Sauls's order, 122–24; from Shaw, 124

Dissention, 128

Education, 5

Election dispute, xi–xii; first filing in, 23; throughout Florida, 47, 105; football compared to, 29; improbability in, 131–32; legislature on, 105–6, 120; political affiliations affecting, 34, 80, 135; prevention related to, 134–35; as process, 135–36; schedule for, 36–37; standards and, 73, 78, 132; subjectivity in, 81–82

Electoral College, 2, 33, 79, 124; deadline for, 36, 63, 76; in Michigan legislature, 112–13; Republican Party for, 105–6, 108–9; selection of, 68, 72–73, 95, 105–6, 108–9, 112–13, 120

Ellege v. Florida, 10

Employment: associations with, 7; civil law in, 9; merit selection in, 7–9; as trial lawyer, 6. *See also* Florida Supreme Court

Family, 5. *See also specific family members*

Federal election statutes, 68–69. *See also* Florida election statutes

Feeney, Tom, 95; against *Armstrong v. Harris*, 105–6

Florida: election dispute throughout, 47, 105; House race in, 6–7; 1970 party politics in, 6–7; Pinellas County, 6, 28, 28n1; political history of, xi; political parties in, x–xi; population of, ix–x; possibilities in, ix; regionalism of, x; World War II and, ix–x

Florida attorney general. *See* Butterworth, Bob

Florida Constitution: death-penalty cases and, 11–12; Death Penalty

Reform Act and, 11; Florida Supreme Court and, 36; jurisdiction and, 40; U.S. Constitution compared to, 18; U.S. Supreme Court on, 113–14

Florida election statutes, 15; Bush, G. W., and, 72–73; conflicts in, 30–31, 64–66; on contest of election, 32, 69–70, 76–77; on deadlines, 23–24, 30–31; Gore and, 72–73, 118–19; history of, 67; intent in, 64–65, 67–69; oral argument for, 81–82; on overseas ballots, 13–15, 14n1; in private conclusion, 87–88; on protest filing, 31; recounts and, 66, 69; U.S. Supreme Court and, 109, 113. *See also specific statutes*

Florida Secretary of State. *See* Harris, Katherine

Florida Statute 102.111, 30, 65–68, 72

Florida Statute 102.112, 30–31, 38, 65–68, 79

Florida Statute 102.166, 31–32, 38

Florida Statute 102.168, 32, 80, 102, 118–19

Florida Supreme Court: *Allen v. Butterworth*, 11, 19; *Armstrong v. Harris*, 11–12, 18–19, 21–22, 105–6; attraction to, 7; bias portrayal of, 44, 44n1; bias reality of, 44–45; clerk's office of, 25; code timeline for, 2, 23–24; confidentiality and, 4; criminal law in, 9–10; criticism of, 110, 128, 134; crowd control at, 26–27, 37, 59, 103; death-penalty cases in, 9–12; dissent from, 3–4, 12, 122–24; division within, 120–24; election dispute schedule for, 36–37; Florida Constitution and, 36; information officer of, 26, 127; judicial labeling of, 17; jurisdiction of, 95–96, 120–21; law clerks in, 14; legislature relationships with, 10–12; liberal label for, 44–45; march to, 102–3; media at, 16–17, 41, 75, 102, 130; merit selection in, 7–9; misinterpretation about, 46–47; nonpartisan status in, 9; original filings in, 40–41; perspective from,

4, 44–45, 63; political affiliations of, 44, 44n1, 92; political problem for, 79; realization for, 35–36, 62–63; for recount, 3, 45–46, 114–15, 122–23; research in, 10; work schedules of, 59. *See also specific justices*

Football, 69; Bowden for, 62, 62n1; election dispute compared to, 29

Fourth District Court of Appeals, 102

Frost, John, 7–8

Gallery, 75

Ginsberg, Benjamin, 71

Gore, Al: actual number of votes for, 131–32; bias portrayal towards, 44, 44n1; brief of, 72–73; concession of, 129; contest of election by, 101–2, 104–5; election win reports on, 1; Florida election statutes and, 72–73, 118–19; lawyers of, 70; recount petition from, 94–97, 106–7; Sauls's order against, 118–19; strategy of, 63

Graham, Bob, 17

Gurney, Ed, 6

Hall, Tom, 13, 24; activities of, 13, 35, 37, 59, 96–97, 106, 110–11, 127, 129; announcement by, 35; background of, 25

Hancock, Paul, 74; deadline from, 76

Harding, Major, 11; background of, 19; dissent from, 124; in oral argument, 77; perspective of, 17; swearing in by, 84–85, 90

Harmless-error analysis, 18

Harris, Katherine, 68; amended returns and, 42–43; appeals rejection by, 42; Butterworth compared to, 35; deadline from, 30, 34, 85; inconsistency of, 67; Lewis, T., and, 38–39, 48; Palm Beach County Canvassing Board and, 45, 99; political affiliations of, 34, 80, 135; political motives of, 71; private conclusion on, 88–89; stay against, 60–61, 80, 88–89. See also *Armstrong v. Harris*; Klock, Joe

Former Florida Supreme Court Chief Justice Charley Wells was born in 1939 in Orlando, where he grew up. He was educated in public schools and graduated from the University of Florida in 1961 and from the University of Florida College of Law in 1964. With the exception of a year spent working in the Civil Division of the U.S. Department of Justice in Washington, D.C. (1969), he was a lawyer in private practice in Orlando from 1965 until June 1994, when he was appointed justice of the Florida Supreme Court. He became chief justice in July 2000 and served in that role until July 2002. He continued as a justice of the Florida Supreme Court until March 2009. He then returned to the private practice of law in Orlando with the law firm GrayRobinson. He is married to Linda Fischer Wells, and they have three children and seven grandchildren.

FLORIDA GOVERNMENT AND POLITICS

Series editors, David R. Colburn and Susan A. MacManus

Florida has emerged today as a microcosm of the nation and has become a political bellwether in national elections. The impact of Florida on the presidential elections of 2000, 2004, and 2008 suggests the magnitude of the state's influence. Of the four largest states in the nation, Florida is the only one that has moved from one political column to the other in the last three national elections. These developments suggest the vital need to explore the politics of the Sunshine State in greater detail. Books in this series will explore the myriad aspects of politics, political science, public policy, history, and government in Florida.

The 57 Club: My Four Decades in Florida Politics, by Frederick B. Karl (2010)

The Political Education of Buddy MacKay, by Buddy MacKay, with Rick Edmonds (2010)

Immigrant Prince: Mel Martinez and the American Dream, by Richard E. Fogelsong (2011)

Reubin O'D. Askew and the Golden Age of Florida Politics, by Martin A. Dyckman (2011)

Red Pepper and Gorgeous George: Claude Pepper's Epic Defeat in the 1950 Democratic Primary, by James C. Clark (2011)

Inside Bush v. Gore, by Charley Wells (2013)